The Damn Good Resume Guide

by Yana Parker

TEN SPEED PRESS

Berkeley, California

The author wishes to acknowledge her colleagues, friends, and clients,
for their assistance, advice, and contributions to this project.
THANK YOU, people!

Copyright © 1983, 1986, 1989 by Yana Parker

1☯

TEN SPEED PRESS
P O Box 7123
Berkeley, California 94707

Cover Design by Brenton Beck and Yana Parker
Illustrations by Ellen Sasaki
Text Design by Hal Hershey

Library of Congress Cataloging-in-Publication Data

Parker, Yana
    The damn good resume guide / by Yana Parker. — Rev.
        p.   cm.
    ISBN 0-898-15-348-4 : $6.95
    1. Résumés (Employment)   I. Title.
  HF5383.P35   1989
    650.14—dc20   89-35640
                                             CIP

Printed in the United States of America

    12   13   14   15   —   96   95   94   93

CONTENTS

How I Came to Write
The Damn Good Resume Guide

LONG-TIME INTEREST

For many years I've had a great interest in people's work lives and job satisfaction (including my own) and this first showed up in a three-year volunteer job as director/coordinator of a community Youth Employment Service. That led to a job with an upstate New York community college project to train "hard-core unemployed youth" (whatever *that* means) in job-related skills, and then on to a similar position as "Community Worker" with New York State employment offices in Albany, Troy, and Schenectady, a job I really loved.

Later, living in California I noticed that many of the people in my personal network were involved in career counseling and small business development, and we'd do brainstorming and strategizing about our own work, just for the fun of it. Then, in 1979, I decided to try self-employment using my writing skills and a new IBM Selectric typewriter; I resigned from office work in the big city to use my talents in a more personally rewarding way. I began by offering an editing, typing, and business writing service out of my home in Oakland, but soon specialized in resumes, because it was "a natural" for me, and because very few people seemed to know how to do it well.

THE HUMBLE FREEBIE GETS STATUS

I never really set out to write or publish this book. It started out, in 1980, as just a few loose pages of instructions and examples, handed to clients as "homework" before we'd get together to work on their resume. (I'd grown weary of verbally giving the same instructions over and over, and finally wrote them down.)

In our "Briarpatch" self-help group of small business people there was a financial consultant, Roger Pritchard, and one day I hired him to help me look critically at the fragile economics of my business. He noticed the packet of "homework" pages I gave to clients (by now it included sample resumes and a list of action verbs), and asked "Why are you *giving* this away? Don't you see that it's valuable, and that you could easily get a few dollars for it?"

So I took his advice, and at the same time expanded the packet and wrote up the instructions in greater detail. I designed a card-stock cover, stapled it together, and priced it at $2. Over the following year it got expanded twice more, and I began to suspect that it might be marketable as a how-to guide independently of my resume writing business. So I typed it up very carefully, added some graphics, designed a more professional cover, and persuaded two local bookstores to carry a few copies on consignment.

GETTING PUBLISHED

It turned out that Phil Wood, owner of Ten Speed Press, almost immediately found a copy in Cody's Bookstore in Berkeley, liked it, and proposed publishing it. Out of negotiations with him and senior editor George Young, it became clear that another section would be helpful: answers to the recurrent problems that come up when people attempt to write a resume. So I wrote that section, called "Ten Tough Questions," based on experience struggling with these dilemmas many times over. The section on employer acceptance, called "The Acid Test," was developed at the suggestion of Richard Bolles, who pointed out the need to be sure that what was presented really did serve the reader in terms of employer expectations.

Now, over five years later, *The Damn Good Resume Guide* has clearly become well respected and popular in its field. Professional job counselors call it "the best available," a fair number of self-help job clubs and career development centers (and even college instructors in psychology, business writing, and women's studies!) have made it "required reading," and people call from some amazing distances asking, "Where can I get a copy?"

THIS NEW EDITION

Since **Damn Good** is so successful and popular, you might ask, "Why fix it? Why a new edition?" The reason is: we want to maintain this book's reputation as a dependable, up-to-date guide; so periodically we are **replacing all the resumes** with more recently written examples that reflect current trends in the world of work, AND **conducting a new survey of employer opinions** about resumes. In this edition we also wanted to add an **index**, add a "**Check List**," and introduce several important new ideas: "The Favorite Skills Alternative," the resume for "Informational Interviewing," and the "Job Upgrade Resume."

The basic concepts and guidelines, however, remain much the same.

THE ROLE OF THE MAGICAL MACINTOSH

In 1984 I began working on a Macintosh computer. Now, looking back at the old days of typewriters seems like looking back at The Dark Ages. I cannot IMAGINE doing my resume work without this wonderful machine. In one-to-one work with job hunters I am now FAR more efficient and productive and creative, and it's more fun. My clients and I write and edit directly on the screen, bypassing paper altogether, and it's wonderful to enjoy the flexibility, speed, and professional appearance made possible by a state-of-the-art word processing tool. In fact, I simply could not do this work without it.

All the resumes in this new edition were produced on the "Mac" and printed on a LaserWriter printer.

Yana Parker
Berkeley, California
Fall, 1989

WHAT <u>IS</u> A DAMN GOOD RESUME?

- **A DAMN GOOD RESUME is a self-marketing tool.**
- **It's designed with one goal in mind: to get you a job interview.**
- **It always starts with a clearly stated Job Objective; then it presents your skills, experience, and accomplishments in terms of THAT current Job Objective.**

This hybrid type of resume combines the best features of "functional," "achievement," and "chronological" resume styles. It is lean, focused, and effective.

In contrast, the old-style standard resume listed your Work History in chronological order (so far so good), but it then went on to describe your old jobs in grim and boring detail, with total disregard for their current relevance. (This was really just a list of abbreviated Job Descriptions.) This old-style resume often OMITTED mention of your current Job Objective (incredible!). And worst of all, it was then left to the hapless potential employer to figure out what all that MEANT to her, what work-role you wanted NOW, and how well suited you were for that position.

A DAMN GOOD RESUME is far more effective because it SELECTS and INTERPRETS your past work experience AS IT RELATES to your current Job Objective. It OMITS everything that isn't clearly relevant to that current objective. It INCLUDES everything that IS clearly relevant—regardless of old job titles (if any) or salary (if any)—giving you full credit for all that you've learned and accomplished.

A DAMN GOOD RESUME is a breath of fresh air to an employer, who looks it over and sighs, "WOW, finally somebody who knows what she wants, who knows what she has to offer, and who gives me *just* the information I really need, in a nice simple form. Terrific!"

A DAMN GOOD RESUME Has Five Essential Parts

1. A clearly stated **Job Objective**
2. The **Highlights of Qualifications**
3. A presentation of directly **Relevant Skills and Experience**
4. A chronological **Work History**
5. A listing of relevant **Education and Training**

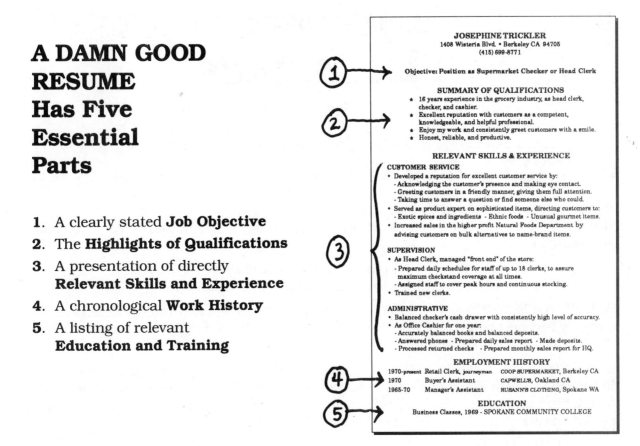

JOSEPHINE TRICKLER
1408 Wisteria Blvd. • Berkeley CA 94705
(415) 699-8771

Objective: Position as Supermarket Checker or Head Clerk

SUMMARY OF QUALIFICATIONS
* 16 years experience in the grocery industry, as head clerk, checker, and cashier.
* Excellent reputation with customers as a competent, knowledgeable, and helpful professional.
* Enjoy my work and consistently greet customers with a smile.
* Honest, reliable, and productive.

RELEVANT SKILLS & EXPERIENCE
CUSTOMER SERVICE
* Developed a reputation for excellent customer service by:
  - Acknowledging the customer's presence and making eye contact.
  - Greeting customers in a friendly manner, giving them full attention.
  - Taking time to answer a question or find someone else who could.
* Served as product expert on sophisticated items, directing customers to:
  - Exotic spices and ingredients - Ethnic foods - Unusual gourmet items.
* Increased sales in the higher profit Natural Foods Department by advising customers on bulk alternatives to name-brand items.

SUPERVISION
* As Head Clerk, managed "front end" of the store:
  - Prepared daily schedules for staff of up to 18 clerks, to assure maximum checkstand coverage at all times.
  - Assigned staff to cover peak hours and continuous stocking.
* Trained new clerks.

ADMINISTRATIVE
* Balanced checker's cash drawer with consistently high level of accuracy.
* As Office Cashier for one year:
  - Accurately balanced books and balanced deposits.
  - Answered phones - Prepared daily sales report - Made deposits.
  - Processed returned checks - Prepared monthly sales report for HQ.

EMPLOYMENT HISTORY
1970-present	Retail Clerk, *journeyman*	COOP SUPERMARKET, Berkeley CA
1970	Buyer's Assistant	CAPWELLS, Oakland CA
1965-70	Manager's Assistant	RUSANN'S CLOTHING, Spokane WA

EDUCATION
Business Classes, 1969 - SPOKANE COMMUNITY COLLEGE

A DAMN GOOD RESUME IS LEAN AND TO-THE-POINT

- It omits detailed descriptions of nonrelevant earlier jobs.
- It omits tiresome jargon like "interfaced" and "responsibilities included."
- It omits the clutter of overly precise dates (we simply say "1984-89").
- It omits all personal information that's not relevant to the job (age, marital status, height, weight, hobbies).

A DAMN GOOD RESUME HELPS OVERCOME PROBLEMS

- It focuses attention on your strong points and accomplishments.
- It minimizes the impact of times when you were unemployed or underemployed.
- It demonstrates that you're a "pro" even if you've never been paid for what you do.
- It shows how you're well qualified for work in a totally new field.

PART ONE

The Basics

GETTING STARTED

START WRITING, using at least five sheets of paper, one for each of the five basic parts of your finished resume:

- Job Objective • Highlights • Relevant Skills and Experience
  • Work History • Education and Training

TYPE UP YOUR NOTES as you go along. A confusing mass of handwritten scraps can suddenly become manageable when it's neatly typed. Keep retyping as you edit, and all at once—VOILA—it takes shape!

SAVE AND FILE ALL YOUR NOTES. This is NOT the last resume you'll ever write; next time it will be much easier using the notes you're now developing. Also, some of the material you generate now will not be relevant for THIS resume, but MAY be relevant for a different version (now or later) when your Job Objective changes.

DO THE FAIRLY EASY PARTS FIRST—the "master lists" of your Work History and your Education and Training—and set those aside. So we'll discuss the process in the following order:

A. Work History
B. Education and Training
C. Job Objective
D. Relevant Skills and Experience
E. Highlights of Qualifications

Advantage of Word Processors

Look at the examples in this book, all word-processed on a Macintosh computer and printed on a LaserWriter printer. You can see that the computer opens up some wonderful new graphic options, and offers great flexibility in type sizes and type faces.

If you are willing to pay a little extra to get your resume word-processed and stored on a disk, then future revisions are low-cost and easy to get in a hurry. These factors can make a big difference. Also, in this day and age, your resume has to stand out against some very sophisticated competition—so I very strongly recommend checking out word-processing in your locality.

A. Work History

First, create a "Work History Master List," keeping in mind that not everything on your "Master List" will necessarily appear on THIS version of your resume. For paid and volunteer jobs or positions, list the dates you started and ended, your job title, and the name and city of the company or organization. Put these jobs in chronological order.

Compare YOUR Work History Master List with the typical resumes in this book. If you have a paid Work History that is fairly short, uncomplicated, and continuous, then you're done with this section. But if it's fragmented, overlapping, too long, too short, nonexistent, or has a large gap in it, then refer to the Sample Resumes and the Ten Tough Questions for ideas on how to deal with each problem.

On your final resume, generally omit months, and simply say "1983-85" or "1986-present." Short periods of unemployment are normal and routine, and go unnoticed in a Work History that sticks to years. (Longer periods out of the work force should be accounted for in a positive statement about what you were doing.)

If a significant part of your work experience came from unpaid/volunteer work, be sure to call this section "Work History" rather than "Employment History."

B. Education and Training

Now create an "Education and Training Master List," this time including:

- schools you attended, with dates, degrees, honors;
- personal study in your field (classes, workshops, and other informal ways you have learned);
- any other credentials or certificates.

For your final resume, select just those items that support your current specific Job Objective, and put THOSE on this current resume. Keep the original master list intact for future reference.

Now the challenging parts!

C. Job Objective

Compose a clearly stated Job Objective, using a minimum number of words.

"OH SURE!," you say, "Just like that!" Take heart, it's NOT just you. EVERYBODY seems to have a hard time being clear and explicit with their Job Objective. It may be the HARDEST part of the resume to do. But it's also critical to be focused here, if your resume is to be effective.

So LIGHTEN UP ABOUT IT. You're not locking yourself into one role for life . . . you only need to be CLEAR about what you want to do NEXT.

Here are some examples of what a clearly stated Job Objective looks like:

- Position as editorial assistant in book publishing.
- Entry position in financial analysis with a major financial institution.
- Position in Administrative Services, focusing on special administrative projects, editing/word processing, and accounts receivable.
- Position as bookstore clerk at Avenue Books.
- General manager in food service, restaurant or food-related business.
- Licensed clinical social worker, specializing in relationship problems and substance abuse, working with individuals, couples, and families.
- Receptionist/office assistant in a chiropractic office.
- Part-time clerical position in a bank.
- Software engineering position with Computer Task Group.
- Trainee in real estate property management.
- Free-lance research, editing, and collaborative writing.
- Position as fire fighter with Berkland City Fire Department.
- Developmental or applications engineer for new plastics products or packaging.
- Position as Director of Industrial Relations with College of San Gabrielle.
- Chemist in a research lab, specializing in hydrocarbon analysis.
- Hypnotherapist in affiliation with a holistic clinic or health center.
- Employment counselor/job development position, working with disabled clients.

Following are two techniques that may help you focus in on your Job Objective. Try #1 first (a method for people who basically know what they want) and if it doesn't work for you then try method #2 (the brainstorm method).

Method #1 - The Question and Answer Method (for stating your objective)

Ask yourself these questions:

- WHAT do I want to do?

- FOR WHOM or WITH WHOM do I want to do it?

- WHERE do I want to do it?

- AT WHAT LEVEL OF RESPONSIBILITY?

For example, suppose you answered this way:

WHAT? . . . teach   FOR WHOM? . . . autistic children

WHERE? . . . in a public school   AT WHAT LEVEL? . . . as head teacher

Then your Job Objective might read, simply and directly:

"Objective: Position as head teacher of autistic children, in a public school."

Write your Job Objective with these tips in mind:

- Your Job Objective is best expressed in the **fewest words possible**, while still being clear and explicit enough to create a mental image of you at work. (An actual job title is extremely effective.)

- Your Job Objective should express the role that you are willing and able to fill, **from the employer's perspective**—what's in it for them, not what's in it for you. Avoid phrases like, ". . . with opportunity for advancement." The interview, not the resume, is the place to talk about what's in it for you.

If Method #1 worked for you, go directly to "Relevant Skills and Experience" on page 13.

Food for Thought

The people who seem to take the longest time to find a job are often the ones who insist on writing a "generic" resume, telling everything they ever did, or every skill they're interested in using, but fail to focus that information onto a specific objective. They HOPE the employer will figure out what job would fit them . . . but employers rarely operate that way.

Method #2 - The Brainstorm Method (for identifying your objective)

You might settle on a Job Objective by starting out with a quick 10-to-15 minute "brainstorm."

• Jot down every job title you can think of that would be acceptable as your very next job. Not necessarily your ideal job or even your job five years from now, but your VERY NEXT job. Don't list "skills used" or "working conditions" either, but actual job titles.

A "brainstorm" list would include every job title that pops into your mind right now, that seems appealing and acceptable . . . given what you already know about those jobs.

• **Prioritize** this "brainstormed" list of job titles by asking yourself these questions:
> —Which job titles realistically belong in the future, after I've gained some more experience?
> —Which of these job interests may more appropriately become my hobbies?
> —**Which ones am I ready for and interested in right NOW?** Of THESE, which would I give first priority? Second priority?

Finally, **select a current Job Objective** from the First Priority group and focus your resume and your job hunt on THAT one for at least the next month.

Here's a "Brainstorm" example from *The Resume Catalog*. Tony, a recent college graduate, did a "brainstorm list" that looked like this **after** we rearranged it according to his **priorities**:

First priority: top interests now
customer services
banking
stockbroker
financial analyst

Second priority:
interest group rep
lobbyist
foreign policy analyst
political specialist
demographer
geographer

Second priority (continued)
travel agent?
politician?
intelligence
defense research
real estate

maybe later, or hobbies
journalist
author
professor, international relations
historian
astronaut?

The current Job Objective Tony settled on was: "Entry position in financial analysis or customer services with a major financial institution."

Then, when a **specific job** came along that he wanted to apply for, he changed it to: "Job Objective: Junior analyst position with Bank of America."

So that's ANOTHER way to go about focusing on your Job Objective.
If this worked for you, move on to "Relevant Skills and Experience" on page 13.

If neither Method #1 nor #2 works for you, and you just don't know what you want to do, try the Favorite Skills Alternative on page 21.

D. Relevant Skills And Experience

Now, here is the heart of your DAMN GOOD RESUME, and it's the most challenging part. Get ready for a radical idea:

> **What we want to create — *contrary* to everything you've heard in the past about resumes — is a *word picture of you in your proposed new job*, created out of the best of your past experience.**

A) So first, get out the sheet of paper on which you've written your current **Job Objective. Ask yourself what are the five or six major skills** required for that job.

B) Get out a sheet of paper **for each of those skills or special knowledge areas, and label each page**. (In some technical fields, special knowledge can be presented in the same way as a skill.) See page 56 for lists of skills and special knowledge.

C) Then **ask yourself, "When did I use those same skills in the past?"**

D) Now on each blank page, **under each of the skills listed, begin to write action-oriented "One-Liner" statements** that clearly and concisely describe how you used or developed those skills in the past.

E) Then you can **assemble the Relevant Skills and Experience section** of your new-job resume by putting those five or six skill paragraphs together on one page.

➔ The illustration on the next two pages shows how one person did this process.

Piece of cake, right?

Now Some Words of Reassurance. It's v-e-r-y easy to get bogged down at this point, in confusion over what to do first, especially if you're less than sure what skills are needed for your new line of work. Some initial chaos here may be inevitable, until you get well into it.

In actual practice working with my resume clients, we often simply GUESS, **tentatively naming some skill areas** that SEEM most relevant to the Job Objective.

Then we begin writing One-Liners, and we SEE if we have enough good material to go under each of those tentative skill headings. Usually we end up rephrasing the skill areas, and/or combining some, and/or breaking some down into two or three other skill areas. **Whew! THIS IS HARD WORK! If you make it this far, you can call yourself an Editor!**

> **TIP: For selecting work experiences to illustrate your skills:**
>
> **Do** choose only work experiences that actually provided a **sense of satisfaction and accomplishment**.
>
> **Don't** focus on just your job duties and responsibilities (i.e., job descriptions). This way you'll have a much more interesting resume, and one that better supports your effort to find a job you'll really ENJOY.

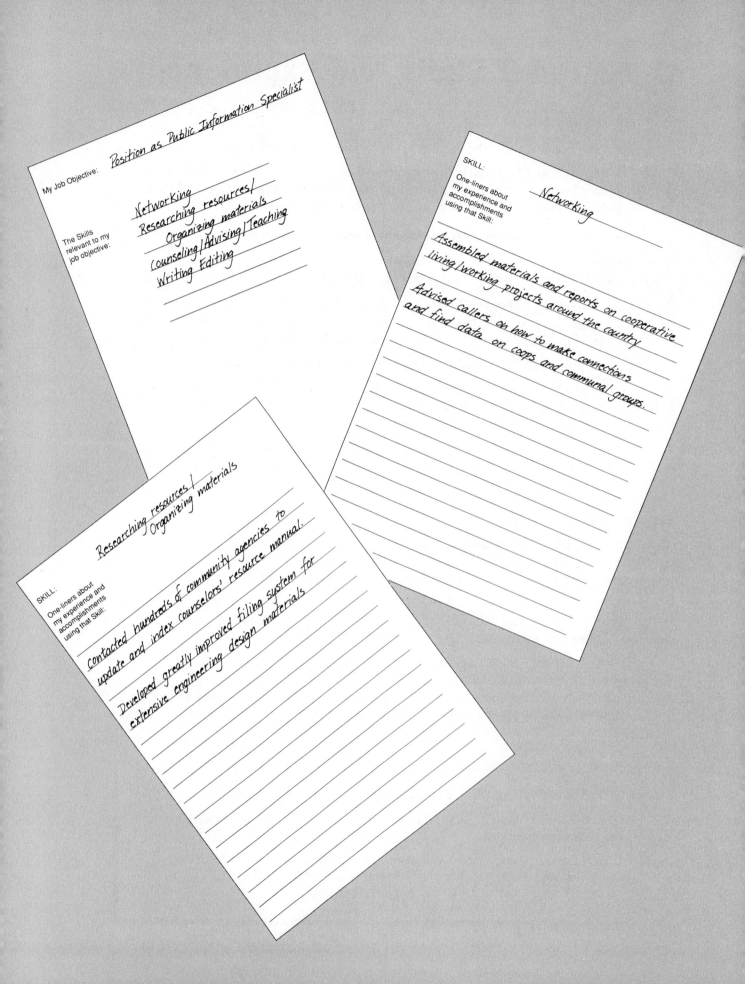

My Job Objective: _Position as Public Information Specialist_

The Skills relevant to my job objective:

Networking
Researching resources/
Organizing materials
Counseling/Advising/Teaching
Writing Editing

SKILL:

One-liners about my experience and accomplishments using that Skill:

Networking

Assembled materials and reports on cooperative living/working projects around the country

Advised callers on how to make connections and find data on coops and communal groups.

SKILL:

One-liners about my experience and accomplishments using that Skill:

Researching resources/
Organizing materials

Contacted hundreds of community agencies to update and index counselors' resource manual.

Developed greatly improved filing system for extensive engineering design materials

Counseling / Advising / Teaching

SKILL:

One-liners about my experience and accomplishments using that Skill:

Consulted with scores of individuals on business writing, teaching them to analyze and present their experience.

Advised people on how to conduct an effective housing search and handle issues, as local resource person for group living.

Taught "Beginning Typing."
Taught "Office Practice."
Taught 6-session "field visits to Bay Area collective homes."

Writing & Editing

SKILL:

One-liners about my experience and accomplishments using that Skill:

Edited book on women's self-led career groups.

Developed series of informative handouts.
Co-authored group self-assessment questionnaire, in widespread local use.

Wrote and self-published instruction manual, "Better Business Letters."

Initiated and produced 12-20 page monthly newsletter for 24 consecutive issues.

MARGO KELLER
3915 Derby Street • Berkeley CA 94705
(415) 390-6554

OBJECTIVE: Public Information Specialist

SUMMARY OF QUALIFICATIONS
- Proven ability to research, identify, and document valuable local resources.
- Skilled and creative writer, with experience in developing effective teaching materials and making public presentations.
- Able to initiate, organize and successfully follow through on projects.

RELEVANT SKILLS & EXPERIENCE

NETWORKING & RESOURCES
- Contacted hundreds of community agencies to update and index EDD Employment Counselors' Resource Manual.
- Assembled library of materials and reports on cooperative living / working projects nationwide; used this to advise callers on how to make connections and find data.
- Developed a greatly improved filing system for extensive archives of design materials for LaRock Engineering.

ADVISING & TEACHING
- Advised hundreds of callers on how to conduct effective housing research and handle related issues, as primary local resource person in collective living field.
- Taught classes in Beginning Typing and Office Practice. Designed and taught a six-session workshop, "Field Visits to Bay Area Collective Homes."
- Consulted with scores of individuals on business writing, teaching them to analyze and present their accomplishments in terms of current goals.

EDITING & WRITING
- Initiated and produced 12-20 page monthly newsletter for 24 consecutive issues.
- Wrote and self-published 50-page instruction manual, "Better Business Letters," approved and used extensively by professionals.
- Edited 100-page book on women's self-led career groups, collaborating with author.
- Co-authored a group self-assessment questionnaire in widespread local use, and developed a series of informative handouts on group problem solving.

EMPLOYMENT HISTORY
1988-now **Keller Business Service** - Self-employed, business typing / editing service
1985-88 **Admin. Asst./Technical Writer** - LaRock Civil Engineers, San Francisco
1984 Travel and independent study
1980-83 **Community Worker** - Local EDD office, NY State Labor Dept., Albany NY
1979-80 **Office Supervisor** - Ager Finance Co., Gloversville NY
1978-79 **Director's Asst. & Instructor** - OEO Job Training Project, Johnstown NY

COMMUNITY SERVICE • CoFounder, Grapevine Cooperative Network, Bay Area

EDUCATION • State University of New York at Albany, 1977-78, Sociology

Tips For Writing One-Liners
describing your relevant skills and experience

SOME DOs and DON'Ts

DOs

1. **Be explicit** and **use action verbs**. BANISH the overworked phrase "Responsible for."

   Employers **don't need a job description**; they need to know **what you accomplished**.
   - "Initiated and wrote a petition signed by 1300 residents to ban nonreturnable bottles, successfully getting it on the ballot."
   - "Taught computer programming to high school students."
   - "Interviewed, hired, and trained 24 waitresses and bartenders."
   - "Self-published a 62-page manual on how to write effective organizational newsletters."

2. **Be "punchy."** Remember that MORE is **NOT** BETTER, and use direct, simple English.

   Say "human relations" instead of "in-ter-per-son-al relations," for example. Two syllables are punchier than five!

3. **Quantify your accomplishments**, where appropriate, telling how much, how many, how often. For example, you can say how many people you supervised, or what your total sales figures were.

4. **Describe the value or benefit** to the company, from your activity, i.e., answer the implied question, **"So What?"** Perhaps your work ultimately saved money, or increased productivity, or improved public relations.

   You may want to use the "Problem-Action-Result" model. A typical "PAR" One-Liner might look like this:

   "Transformed a chaotic, inefficient warehouse into a smooth-running operation by totally redesigning the layout, saving the company $250,000 in recovered stock."

5. **Take credit for your role** in the activity. If it was a team effort, you can say "Coauthored . . . " or "Collaborated with . . . " or "Co-led . . . "

6. **Describe the accomplishment so it is clear what your contribution was.** For example:
   - Supervised the entire relocation project of our company's satellite warehouse, successfully moving $6 million in equipment and material in one weekend:
     - computed the best layout of floor space to assure a smooth flow of materials;
     - set up a computerized inventory location system.
   - Earned public recognition for outstanding project management of an important scientific study involving new uses for chemical waste products:
     - trained other technicians in correct research methods;
     - carefully monitored data and alerted engineers to any inconsistencies;
     - maintained consistent procedures to guarantee the integrity of the research.

7. **Use COMPOUND One-Liners**, as in the example above, to describe an accomplishment involving several different steps. A Compound One-Liner starts off

with a fairly general overview statement, ending in a colon, and followed by several more detailed sub-statements. This gives you the chance to use even MORE action verbs, one at the beginning of each line. Notice how many action verbs are used above: "supervised," "computed," "set up," "earned recognition," "trained," "carefully monitored," "maintained." — all in just two Compound One-Liners.

DON'Ts

1. **Don't take your accomplishments for granted.** Perhaps you resolved a long-standing problem, or discovered a new and better approach to getting things done.

2. **Don't be modest** about saying that you're good at what you do. Perhaps you were just doing what you were supposed to do, but if you did it with pride and professionalism, and got excellent results, that **does** matter.

3. **Don't be constrained by the "official" job descriptions or responsibilities**, when describing your work accomplishments. Sometimes you do your most valuable and creative work when you're operating BEYOND or outside routine expectations.

4. Keep referring back to your Job Objective and **don't describe activities that are not in any way relevant to it.**

5. **Don't describe ANY work experience you didn't like**, or want to avoid repeating in your new job. (*Really!*)

HERE ARE SOME EXAMPLES OF SKILLS AND ONE-LINERS
(The last one is a variation we call a "Compound One-Liner.")

Skill: Marketing (the objective was Sales in the food industry)
- Developed a highly successful label identity for Paradise Foods (which previously had none), now universally recognized as synonymous with top quality products.
- Pioneered a very popular special pack in metric weight to address the needs and expectations of the European market, which was so popular that it set an industry packing standard for that product.

Skill: Resource Development (the objective was Director of a housing agency)
- Prepared a clear, easily understood self-help manual on eviction and eviction-defense, for both landlords and tenants.
- Assembled a comprehensive Referral Guide to community resources on housing and legal services.

Special Knowledge: Technical Expertise (the objective was Engineering Customer Service)
- Collaborated in the successful design of an ignition system for a high-mileage vehicle, in a competition sponsored by the Society for Automotive Engineers.
- Developed a unique and economical design for a spectrophotometer, incorporating a special optical line-scanner chip requiring less hardware.

Skill: Events Coordinating (the objective was Meeting Coordinator)
- Coordinated registration of 1500 people for SEVA's special conference:
  —Received and recorded fees, maintaining records on computerized database.
  —Wrote and mailed confirmation letters summarizing participant information.
  —Supervised 7 assistants in handling correspondence and ticketing.
  —Oversaw staffing of registration tables.
  —Screened scholarship applicants and selected scholarship recipients.
  —Wrote critique reporting on the conference registration procedures.

E. The Highlights of Qualifications

This could also be called: "Summary of Qualifications," or simply "Summary."

This is my very favorite section of the resume, because it is the one section that can immediately draw attention and make your resume stand out from all the others. It's a unique paragraph that is unabashedly **self-marketing**.

The essential message of the Highlights is two-fold:

1) First, that you are QUALIFIED — you have the experience, credentials, and basic skills needed for the job.

2) Second, that you are also ESPECIALLY TALENTED (perhaps even gifted) in the areas that really matter — in other words, for THIS job, you're "hot."*

> *Now I can hear some of you muttering, "Oh, but I'm not sure I'm **really** 'hot.' In which case you've almost certainly got the **wrong Job Objective**, and then **of course** you wouldn't be hot at **that**! So look again at what you're really "hot" at, what gives you great satisfaction and a sense of worth and joy and accomplishment, and then reconsider your Job Objective accordingly.

And that's a winning combination: basically qualified PLUS unique and special.

All the REST of the resume, of course, needs to be consistent with the generalizations made in these Highlights, backing them up with facts and figures, telling what, when, where, and how.

The primary advantage of using the Highlights section is that you can MAKE SURE the reader gets the essential points you're trying to present. Your Name/Address, Objective, and Highlights — all by themselves — are like a "mini resume." If THAT MUCH captures the attention of your reader, they're more likely to read further for the details of your skills and experience.

HOW TO WRITE A GOOD "HIGHLIGHTS OF QUALIFICATIONS"

My favorite approach is the **Best-Friend Scenario** method.

First imagine this scene: A really special friend of yours, who knows you very well and knows just what your strengths and special qualities are, JUST HAPPENS to also be professionally acquainted with the Hiring Person at the firm where you'd like to work! (*A fortuitous coincidence.*)

Your Best Friend sincerely thinks you'd be just perfect for the employer's job opening. They are having lunch, and your Best Friend says to the Hiring Person: "Listen, I know the very woman for that job, and you'd be *crazy* not to hire her. She's got everything you're looking for."

And your Best Friend rattles off five hard-hitting, true, appreciative statements about you. These describe your qualifications and strengths so succinctly and persuasively that the Hiring Person is most impressed, and responds, "Well, SURE I want to meet her. Sounds good to me!"

Now, **what WERE those five hard-hitting, true, appreciative statements** your friend put forth? Whatever they were, **that's what should be in your Highlights**.

A typical group of Highlights might include:

    a) How much relevant **experience** you have.
    b) What your formal training and **credentials** are, if relevant.
    c) One significant **accomplishment**, very briefly stated.
    d) One or two outstanding **skills** or abilities.
    e) A reference to your **values**, commitment, or philosophy if appropriate.

Here are three examples of Highlights (and their corresponding Job Objectives):

Objective: Position as Radio Programmer — Third World and Special Projects

★ 12 years experience producing programs on the cutting edge, provoking new understanding of science, art, music, and history.
★ Influential in introducing black avant-garde music to the Bay Area.
★ Recognized authority in the field of third world creative programming.
★ Conceptual talent for clarifying and developing the essence of a project.
★ Demonstrated commitment to supporting integrity and creativity in media.

Objective: Position as Professional Waiter with a unique, quality restaurant.

★ Attuned to the working rhythms of the restaurant business, and able to see what is required at any point in time.
★ Professional talent for assessing and adapting to the moods and needs of both restaurant guests and other staff.
★ Highly creative in resolving problems and developing profitable opportunities.
★ Enthusiastic and persuasive in promoting a quality product.
★ Sharp, hard working, and productive.

Objective: Position in Marketing, Public Relations, and/or Promotions.

★ A "born promoter," able to generate enthusiasm in others.
★ Proven successful in increasing sales and customer base.
★ 10 years experience in public relations and promotions.
★ Extremely well organized; follow through to the last detail.
★ Balanced strengths in careful listening and decisive action taking.
★ Committed to producing results above and beyond what's expected.

Look at the Highlights (or Summaries) on the resumes in this book for more ideas. However, **please do not copy someone else's Highlights** verbatim! It will not do you justice. Even if everything they say about themselves is also true about you, **that's not the point!** Those are the most important highlights for THAT person for THAT objective, and there's no way this can be identical for YOU with YOUR particular objective. Besides, *The Damn Good Resume Guide* gets around. At least one reader was embarrassed when he got caught using another person's Highlights directly from this book. Don't let it happen to you!

... and finally: **Putting It All Together**

FIRST DRAFT

Assemble the five parts of your resume—Job Objective, Highlights, Relevant Experience, Work History, Education—and type up a draft copy. Better yet, word-process it. This draft should LOOK like it's ready to go, even though there's still another step: **getting feedback**.

Omit anything personal and unrelated to your Job Objective (age, marital status, height/weight, hobbies). It's true that some of this personal information will be of interest to the employer, but let that come out in the INTERVIEW. Don't include personal information on the resume because it MAY cause you to be unfairly screened out BEFORE the interviews, on the basis of just one person's prejudice.

Omit the details of less important past jobs that create an image you don't want to take with you. A resume is NOT a confessional! It's your personal marketing document, designed expressly to present you in the most favorable light.

Keep it to one page if you can. This is much easier to accomplish with a computer or word processor than with a standard typewriter. Look at the sample resumes as a guide to the minimum amount of white space you need. If your resume is too crowded, it will turn off the reader and it won't work to your benefit. Employers would rather see two pages than one that's overcrowded.

If your resume is on two pages:
a) Present your "aces" on page one (job objective, skills, accomplishments)
b) Use page two for the work history and education.
c) Be sure to write "continued" on page one, and "page two" PLUS your full name on the second page.
d) Print it on two sheets of paper, and don't staple them together (the two pages can then be placed side-by-side to view the whole resume at once.)

Consult the "Check List for a Damn Good Resume" on page 76.

FINAL VERSION

Get feedback. Show this draft to your most knowledgeable friends, coworkers, and family, and ask them how it "feels." Ask for ideas on improving the wording or layout. (You may need to remind them that your resume is about you at your BEST.)

Type a final version, considering the best of the feedback you got. Give it one last review, using the **"Check List"** again.

THE FAVORITE SKILLS ALTERNATIVE

or "Informational Interviewing Resume"

Writing a Resume when you DON'T know your Job Objective but you DO know what you like to do.

Are you still vague and fuzzy about your Job Objective?

Don't despair!

Maybe you can develop your resume using a two-part alternative that starts with past experiences where you used your favorite skills.

WARNING: You'll have to go all the way with this one. It won't work to have a resume with just your favorite skills on it; it also has to have a job focus.

KNOW YOURSELF

Start off by **identifying** some of your most satisfying work experiences, those that gave you a sense of **accomplishment** and **satisfaction**.

> Keep always in mind that work-is-work-is-work, and "good work" is not necessarily or always "paid work"; if it was valuable and productive, it counts as "work."

Create One-Liners that **describe** those satisfying experiences and accomplishments. (See "Tips For Writing One-Liners" on page 16.) For example,

> "Taught my boss and coworkers how to use the new computer in our office, and then wrote a manual of instructions for new employees."

Then, look at each experience and **write down what skills you were using** in each case. In the example above, it might be "teaching" and "writing." For more ideas, there's a long list of skills on page 56.

Notice that some patterns emerge, and you tend to use the same skills over and over, even though the situations may be quite different.

Now **group together all the experiences that used the same or similar skills**.

Next, take a stab at summarizing what **work role you could fill** using those skills. (*Come on, you can do it!*) The person above might say:

> "*Objective:* Writing and editing position with a publisher or software company involving word processing, teaching/training, and knowledge of PCs."

NOW you have a TENTATIVE objective, and some One-Liners (in skill groups) that illustrate what you've already accomplished using your favorite skills.

Add your Work History and Education, and assemble a draft resume. (See "Putting It All Together," page 20, and "Checklist," page 76.)

BUT . . . that's only the FIRST part! Now, with this preliminary or "Informational Interviewing" resume in your pocket, you need to **go out and . . . (tah-dah) . . .**

KNOW THE WORLD OF WORK

Do some research. Find out what's going on out there, and what jobs you might find (or create) that use these favorite skills. This is a very major task, so do not hesitate to get all the help you can from your friends, family, local employment office, community college, and library.

> — At the library, consult the *Dictionary of Occupational Titles.*

> — Among your working acquaintances, and THEIR acquaintances, **do some "informational interviewing"** (described on page 23) for leads on how you could use those favorite skills.

> — Show people your draft resume for feedback on how to improve it.

> — Explore in every possible direction for ways to apply those favorite skills.

THEN you can come back and **finalize your resume:**

> — Insert an appropriate, specific Job Objective, and . . .

> — Review and fine-tune the One-Liners describing your work experience and skills.

INFORMATIONAL INTERVIEWING

(From *The Resume Catalog*, by Yana Parker)

WHAT IS INFORMATIONAL INTERVIEWING?

"Informational Interviewing" is career counselor jargon for the process of **systematically researching your career field** through a series of in-person workplace visits with people already employed in similar jobs. It is one of the most valuable career development tools.

WHAT'S IN IT FOR ME?

Some major benefits of informational interviewing are:

• It **demystifies** the field or position you're interested in, making it easier to . . .
   — speak knowledgeably about what you want to do, and
   — decide whether this is really an appropriate career choice.

• It provides you with explicit **job description information** that you need in developing a sharp and focused resume, and a source of **constructive criticism** if you've brought a draft resume with you.

• It contributes **valuable personal contacts** for your job search networking, which is the time-tested, surest route to a good job.

HOW DO I GO ABOUT IT?

Some guidelines about informational interviewing:

1. **Don't confuse it with a Job Interview** (in fact you might better call it "career research" to avoid misunderstandings). Be clear, honest, and unambiguous about your motive or agenda, and stick to the agenda of just getting career information, not fishing for a job opening.

2. **Make an explicit appointment** for a short period of time (say 20 minutes); be on time, and leave on time.

3. **Arrive thoroughly prepared** with the questions you want answered.

4. **Leave with at least two referrals** to other people in the field that you can talk to in the same way.

5. **Take down notes immediately** after the interview, recording everything you learned.

6. **Send a thank-you note** right away.

7. **Keep well-organized records** of your informational interviewing process.

HOW DO I FIND PEOPLE TO TALK TO?

• Ask your friends and acquaintances, "Who do you know who works at a job SOMETHING LIKE the one I'm looking for?" Then ask THOSE PEOPLE, "Who do you know who works at a job JUST LIKE the one I'm looking for?"

That's the most direct way; another is:

• Check with a local career counseling center — perhaps a nonprofit agency or a community college placement center — for leads on people available for informational interviewing.

PART TWO

22 Sample Resumes

The following are actual resumes of real people with whom the author has worked; nothing has been made up, but some of the names and details have been changed at the job hunter's request.

All these resumes were produced on an Apple Macintosh computer and printed on a LaserWriter printer in a variety of fonts.

Word-processed resumes, like these, have become commonplace and offer a great advantage over traditional typewriting or typesetting: they're a cinch to revise and update frequently at minimal cost.

BALINDA JACKSON

2222 - 47th Ave., Apt. D
Oakland, CA 94601
(415) 122-8907

Objective: Position as Secretary/Receptionist,
preferably involving information services and a high level of public contact.

HIGHLIGHTS OF QUALIFICATIONS

★ Highly dependable, punctual, and efficient.
★ Supportive team worker; committed and responsible.
★ Able to prioritize workload and meet deadlines.
★ Thrive in a high-energy environment.
★ Experience working in various ethnic settings.

RELEVANT EXPERIENCE

Phones - Public Contact - Information Services

- Answered and redirected incoming calls at:
  ...County Housing Authority   ...State Health Dept.
  ...Macy's Dept. Store   ...Unemployment Office.
- Advised tenants on employment opportunities and local sources of financial assistance, as Housing Assistant with Contra Costa County.
- Referred single parents to emergency community services, including food stamps, financial support, health services, legal aid, and child care.
- Handled high volume of call-ins at Suicide Prevention, a hot-line crisis center.

Administrative Support

- Ordered lab equipment, office supplies, and chemicals for state health department.
- As Housing Assistant with Contra Costa County:
  ...maintained personnel records
  ...calculated subsidized rents of low-income families
  ...conducted inspections of dwellings
  ...prepared legal documents, such as eviction papers
  ...conferred with landlords on fair market rents.

Word Processing - Typesetting

- Operated a range of office machines:
  ...IBM word processor ...AB Dick printer ...AM Varitype typesetter ...10-key adding machine

EMPLOYMENT HISTORY

1988-present	**Receptionist**	H&R BLOCK, Oakland CA
1986-87	**Housing Assistant**	CONTRA COSTA CO. HOUSING AUTHORITY, Richmond CA
1985-86	**Housing Clerk**	CONTRA COSTA CO. HOUSING AUTHORITY, Richmond CA
1985	**Office Assistant II**	STATE HEALTH DEPT., Virus Lab, Berkeley CA
1981-84	**Word Processor**	STATE HEALTH DEPT., Administration, Berkeley CA
1980-81	**Office Assistant**	UNEMPLOYMENT OFFICE, Oakland CA
1976-79	**Sales Rep**	MACY'S, Richmond CA

EDUCATION

Ongoing studies at San Francisco State University

PAUL NYGREN
1350 Maple St., #105
San Francisco CA 94109`
(415) 309-8676

Objective: Position as Group Operations Manager, with a focus on increasing market share and outperforming the competition through exceptional guest service and innovative management strategies.

HIGHLIGHTS OF QUALIFICATIONS

★ 18-year professional background in the hotel field, including international experience in both operations and consulting.

★ Expertise in team-building and organizational development; thorough understanding of how various departments interrelate.

★ Solid understanding of service as the product of the total organizational process.

★ Reputation for ethical relationships with staff and guests.

★ Successful at involving the entire staff in implementing the marketing plan.

PROFESSIONAL EXPERIENCE & ACCOMPLISHMENTS

OPERATIONS

• Developed and implemented a **sales and marketing driven management strategy**, enabling a new property, the Pan Pacific Singapore Hotel, to successfully compete in a fiercely competitive environment.

• As **General Manager for two hotels:**
(San Francisco Suites; and The Charter, a luxury resort in Vail CO)
-Initiated greatly **improved operating systems**, resulting in smoother hotel operations, improved staff morale, and better quality customer service.
-Introduced **state-of-the-art organizational models**, allowing hotel staff to develop a new understanding of their relationship to the guest.

• In 9 years with Marriott Hotels, Rooms Division:
-**Opened a new hotel** in Washington DC, overseeing recruiting and training for the staff of 100, and developing operating procedures for the front office.
-Earned consistent promotions, ultimately handling three Marriott properties.

HUMAN RESOURCE DEVELOPMENT (HRD)

• As Director of HRD for the Pan Pacific Singapore Hotel:
-**Developed a recruitment plan** to attract and select a staff of 800 people in a full employment economy.
-**Designed the training facilities** and organization-wide training plan for 800 people, with a focus on sales skills and exceptional guest service.

• **Designed the regional training center** for 1200-room Hyatt Hotel, Singapore.

• **Co-designed a training model** for Marriott Hotels, to be used in their front office departments. **Results:**
-Improved the staff selection process.
-Reduced staff turnover.
-Accelerated and strengthened the management development process.

- Continued -

PAUL NYGREN
Page two

SALES & MARKETING

- **Implemented innovative, workable systems** that enabled all guest contact staff to play an active, supportive role in the sales and marketing process.
- **Reorganized** a hotel front office under the sales and marketing department, greatly **improving interdepartmental communication** and **increasing sales.**
- **Successfully marketed** a resort to local businesses, resulting in approximately $60,000 referral business within a 3-month period.

FINANCE

- **Developed realistic and workable budgets** of up to $700,000, for both departments and entire properties.
- **Created training budgets** for hotels and for a regional center, to provide training for hundreds of staff at all levels.
- Performed daily accounting functions: journals, general ledger, bill paying, budgeting.

HOTEL OPENINGS

- **Opened** a 400-room Marriott **flagship hotel,** as Front Office Manager overseeing a staff of 100.
- Served as **HRD Director** for the **pre-opening phase** of an 800-room, five-star international hotel.
- Acted as **Interim General Manager** for an exclusive $80 million resort during pre-opening, at the request of the lender.

CONSULTING

- Conducted **Guest Service Critiques,** enabling hotel management to identify strengths and areas to improve, and to implement strategies for change.
- **Co-developed** and conducted a 5-week **course on effective meeting skills,** successfully adopted for use by several different companies.
- **Trained key managers** in small groups and one-on-one, to improve their individual and team **leadership skills.**
- Conducted a **training needs analysis** for a 1200-room Hyatt, and followed through with an **organization-wide training plan and training process.**

EMPLOYMENT HISTORY

1986-present	**General Manager**	SAN FRANCISCO SUITES, time-share hotel
1985-86	**President/Co-owner**	CENTER FOR EXCELLENCE, management consulting co.
1984-85	**Director, Human Resource Development**	PAN PACIFIC SINGAPORE HOTEL, Singapore
1981-84	**President**	CENTER FOR EXCELLENCE, U.S. and Singapore
1971-80	**Rooms Div. Manager**	MARRIOTT CORP., Philadelphia and Washington DC

EDUCATION

B.S., Hotel Administration - UNIVERSITY OF NEW HAMPSHIRE, 1970

PROFESSIONAL AFFILIATIONS
•Hotel Sales and Marketing Assoc., International
•San Francisco Hotel Council •American Resort and Residential Development Assoc.

KATE DIETRICH

4877 Twin Oaks Road
Berkeley CA 94707
(415) 885-9090

Kate aims for an accounting job that allows her to apply her knowledge of computers. Kate's cover letter is on page 61.

Objective: Position with a microcomputer firm, in accounting/bookkeeping.

HIGHLIGHTS OF QUALIFICATIONS

★ Over 12 years experience in accounting, taxation, and administration for a variety of businesses.
★ Over 4 years full-charge bookkeeping experience with computerized accounting systems.
★ Familiar with both PC-DOS and Macintosh operating systems.
★ Exceptionally organized and resourceful, with a wide range of skills.
★ Reliable and adaptable; learn new systems quickly, and take initiative.

RELEVANT EXPERIENCE & ACCOMPLISHMENTS

Accounting/Bookkeeping

- Handled full-charge bookkeeping for 20 accounts monthly at a CPA firm. Calculated payroll taxes, sales taxes, financial statements, depreciation schedules, and Schedule C for each firm.
- Developed a broad base of experience in bookkeeping for a range of businesses including auto repair facilities, service industries, wholesale manufacturing, retail stores, and property management.
- 12 years accounts payable experience. Solely managed up to $75,000 a month in accounts payable.
- Over 15 years experience preparing payroll for up to 60 employees on a weekly basis. Computed, prepared, paid and filed all federal and state tax returns.
- Conducted extensive research of source documents to accurately construct a corporation's first year financial statement and general ledger.

Computer Expertise

Accounting
- Maintained accounting records for 20 businesses, using a custom accounting package on a WANG computer. Generated financial statements, payroll taxes, and W-2 forms.
- Generated financial statements and general ledger for a retail corporation, using New England Business Systems accounting package.

Systems & Applications
- Used LOTUS 1-2-3, WORD PERFECT and Microsoft WORD on an IBM-PC to generate spreadsheets and correspondence.
- Used dBase on an IBM-PC to design custom screens, generate reports, design menus, and design program sub-routines.
- Used Microsoft WORKS and Microsoft WORD on a Macintosh to generate spreadsheets and correspondence for an attorney.
- Generated coding and entered data on an IBM-PC for output to a photo-typesetter.

EMPLOYMENT HISTORY

1987-present	Administrative Assistant*	DOUGLAS HILL, Attorney, Berkeley
1987-present	Bookkeeper/Office Manager*	GRIFFIN MOTORWERKE, Berkeley
1986-87	Customer Service Rep	COLORCRAFT, Inc. (printing) Milwaukee WI
1985-86	Quality Control Assistant	M.C.P. Co. (printing) Milwaukee WI
1984	Real Estate Association	WAUWATOSA REALTY, Hales Corners WI
1982-83	Full Charge Bookkeeper	EDWIN DONAHUE, CPA, El Cerrito
1976-81	Bookkeeper/Parts Manager	AUTOWERKE, Inc. (auto repair/parts) Berkeley
	* concurrently	

EDUCATION & TRAINING

A.A. Degree, with honors - **Printing and Publishing Operations**
Milwaukee Area Technical College, 1985-86
dBase - Vista College, Berkeley
Concepts of Data Processing, Accounting - UC Extension, Berkeley

STEPHEN SEUFERT

1855 Woodside Road, Apt.206
Redwood City CA 94061
(415) 908-6773

Shortly after high school graduation, Stephen has only minimal work experience, so he strengthens his resume with relevant skills gained in a variety of other ways — through classwork, odd jobs, and even helping around home.

Current job objective:Entry position with a computer manufacturer.
Longer-term goal: Position in advertising, sales, and marketing of computer products.

SUMMARY

★ Energetic, hard working, willing to learn and
  accept constructive criticism.
★ Strong motivation for advancing in a career.
★ Enjoy contributing to a team effort and creating
  a good working environment.
★ Basic understanding of the Macintosh computer.

RELEVANT SKILLS & EXPERIENCE

Maintenance Skills
• As carpenter's helper:
  -painted interior walls -measured and cut lumber -helped with framing
  -operated power tools (saws, drills, sanders).
• Did basic home maintenance:
  -rewired lamps -repaired plumbing and appliance -built shelves.
• Completed classes in:
  -electronics (built a TV scrambler from a circuit board)
  -architectural drafting -basic carpentry.

Office Support Skills
• Assisted in inventory control and priced merchandise, as stock clerk at
  Robert's Market.
• Cashiered at Robert's, computing and handling large sums of money.
• Answered phones as needed.
• Completed class in Marketing:
  -invented unique products
  -developed simulated marketing strategies.

Computer Familiarity
• Basic understanding of Macintosh programs, MacWrite and MacPaint.

WORK HISTORY

Dec '87-Jan '88 **Stock Clerk/Cashier** ROBERT'S MARKET, Woodside CA

Summer 1985* **Valet Parking Asst.** MENLO COUNTRY CLUB, Woodside CA

(* while in school) Plus short-term jobs as Carpenter's Helper, Waiter, Busboy, Stockwork.

EDUCATION

Woodside High School, Woodside CA, 1987

MIREYA ORT
Miraflores #14
Berkeley CA 94708
(415) 907-3434

Objective: Position as psychotherapist in a mental health and/or substance abuse program, working with individuals, couples, families, or groups.

EDUCATION
M.A., Clinical Psychology, 1987
License-eligible MFCC Registered Intern No. IB-12499
John F. Kennedy University Graduate School of Professional Psychology, Orinda CA
B.A., Zoology, College of the Pacific, Stockton CA, 1957; 4 year scholastic scholarship

AFFILIATIONS
California Association of Marriage and Family Therapists
Bicultural Association of Spanish Speaking Therapists and Advocates
Interamerican Society of Psychology

PROFESSIONAL EXPERIENCE

Current **PRIVATE PRACTICE**
With individuals, couples, families, groups (SPANISH/ENGLISH)
Office of Carmen Silvia Palacio, Ph.D., Licensed Clinical Psychologist, Berkeley CA
Psychotherapist/Registered Intern

1965-now **MERRITT HOSPITAL**, Oakland CA
All lab shifts and departments.
Licensed Medical Lab Technologist

1987-88 **CONTRA COSTA COUNTY MENTAL HEALTH**
Partial Hospital Intensive Day Treatment Program, Richmond CA
Individual, Family, Group Therapy Intern
Dual Diagnosis Training for NIMN-funded pilot project.

1986-87 **SAN FRANCISCO GENERAL HOSPITAL**
UC Intergenerational Family Therapy Project (NIDA-funded)
Contextual Family Therapist Trainee and Research Assistant
Coauthored and presented symposium on procedures and outcomes at the Congress of
Interamerican Psychology, Havana, Cuba, 1987.

1985-86 **CLINICA de la RAZA COMMUNITY HEALTH CENTER**
Outpatient Mental Health Services, Oakland CA
Psychotherapist Trainee

1974-79 **CREATIVE LIVING CENTER** (Mental Health Day Program), Berkeley CA
HIGHLAND HOSPITAL PSYCHIATRIC UNITS, Oakland CA
Volunteer Staff (in-service training)

1962-63 **PEACE CORPS TRAINING PROGRAM**, UC Berkeley
Instructor on Panamanian Culture and Traditions

- Continued on page two -

HIGHLIGHTS OF QUALIFICATIONS

- **Bilingual, multicultural** personal and professional background.
- Strong in **problem-focused** interventions and **engagement** of resistant clients.
- Skilled in working collaboratively with professional **treatment teams.**
- Specialist in contextual, family systems, and object relations modalities.
- Experience with the following:
  - Intake interviews; clinical assessment; referrals; treatment plans.
  - **DSM III disorders** including major affective, psychoses, substance abuse or addiction.
  - **Immigration** and intergenerational conflicts.
  - Young adult and women's groups issues.
  - **Dual diagnosis** (mental dysfunction and chemical dependence).
  - Advocating and interpreting for clients with **community service agencies,** such as case managers, conservators, medical/legal/housing agencies, probation officers, Child Protective Service, schools, Vocational Rehabilitation.
  - Use of a variety of modes and **therapeutic tools:**
    ...psychoeducation ...psychodrama ...videotape ...one-way mirror
    ...assertiveness training ...independent living skills training.

RELEVANT WORKSHOPS & TRAINING

The Incorporation of Cultural Aspects in Family Therapy
Strategic Therapy for Abuse in the Family: Sexual, Physical, Drug.
Stress in the Latino Community: Resources and Interventions
Contextual Family Therapy of Drug Abuse: Theoretical Models and Clinical Applications
Recognition, Assessment and Treatment of the Dual Diagnosis Client
Positive Confrontation with Substance Abusers
Family Reconstruction Following Immigration
Psychodrama for the Working Practitioner
Principles and Process of Diagnosis with the DSMIII-R

Mireya revised her draft resume to incorporate the feedback she got from her colleagues and supervisors, presenting her education first and highlighting her workplaces because she was fortunate to have outstanding field placements during her training.

ADELE MARTIN
30089 "E" Street
Sacramento CA
(405) 366-1121

You might choose to leave off the "Education" section, as Adele did, so as not to draw attention to it when you have neither any college education nor any training courses to list on your resume.

Objective: Contract Administrator with Travis Air Force Base.

HIGHLIGHTS OF QUALIFICATIONS

★ Ten years experience in contract administration.
★ Excellent presentation skills; clear and professional manner.
★ Able to maintain a balanced, objective viewpoint in addressing problems.
★ Enjoy the challenge of new projects and handling several priorities at once.
★ Consistently earned outstanding performance evaluations and awards.
★ Effective in managing a harmonious staff of ethnic and cultural diversity.

RELEVANT SKILLS & EXPERIENCE

CONTRACT DEVELOPMENT

* Managed all aspects of the contract process:
  -RFP writing and review -Contract awards -Negotiation -Quality assurance plans
  -Maintenance of contract file -Termination -Retirement.

* Represented the government's position when contract challenges occurred, with consistent success.

* Interpreted and clarified daily work activities to fulfill contract requirements:
  -Maintained direct communication with operations managers and key staff to assure accurate overview of activity and ensure contract integrity.

* Facilitated a continuous refinement of contract terms and details over the life of the contract (lasting as much as 6 years):
  -Identified operational obstacles that could interfere with deadlines.
  -Developed workflow patterns to increase product quality.
  -Initiated "meet and deal" meetings; led discussions, created solutions.

* Analyzed quality assurance reports, productivity measurements, and contract specifications prior to archiving and retirement of contract documents.

GENERAL MANAGEMENT

* Assisted in defining agency's mission, goals, and objectives, as Deputy Regional Administrator and Branch Chief.

* Advised Regional Administrator:
  -Formulated policy and procedures.
  -Directed logistical support: budget, staffing, short/long-term planning, training.

* Continuously reassessed workload priorities to meet the stated objectives:
  -Managed budget, requested and justified additional funding.
  -Developed cost-saving recommendations for staffing and outside contracting.
  -Assessed staffing patterns to assure compliance with EEO requirements.

EMPLOYMENT HISTORY

1974-present   **U.S. VETERANS ADMINISTRATION,** San Francisco
Deputy Regional Administrator, GM-13
Branch Chief/Contractor Support, GS-12
Branch Chief/Program Officer, GS-12
Supervisory Claims & Collections Specialist, GS-12
Contract Monitor Specialist, GS-11
Branch Chief/Supervisory Management Analyst, GS-1
Branch Chief/Supervisory Computer Technician, GS-09
Account Examiner, GS-07

KATHLEEN ALLISON
3770 Keystone Ave., #207
Los Angeles CA 90034
(213) 558-0805

Like Adele, Kathleen omits the "Education" section because all her career training comes from on-the-job experience.

Objective: Position in the travel or hotel industry:
•Sales •Public Relations •Promotion

SUMMARY OF QUALIFICATIONS

★ Successfully increased travel consortium membership from 40 to 130 in five months, as Regional Sales Manager.
★ 3 years experience working major trade shows, both as buyer and seller.
★ Proven skill in organizing and managing a territory for maximum efficiency.
★ Developed effective working relationships with travel agency owners and staff.
★ Highly motivated; committed to delivering top quality service.
★ Skilled in use of PCs and Eastern's SystemOne program.

RELEVANT SKILLS & EXPERIENCE

SALES/PRESENTATIONS

As Regional Sales Manager with SPACE & LEISURE travel consortium, increased regional membership of the consortium from 40 to 130:
• Conducted successful membership drive featuring dinner seminars:
-Planned and organized all logistics, including negotiation of space, developing menu, and guest list.
-Delivered "benefits" portion of sales presentation to agency owners.
-Followed up with a personal call to each owner, and closed sales.

TERRITORY MANAGEMENT

Revitalized the dormant southeast territory of SPACE & LEISURE:
• Called on existing members and reestablished relationships with them.
• Researched the needs of individual agencies, and collaborated with marketing department on customized programs offering a needed competitive edge.
• Selected candidates for an Advisory Board of top agency owners; participated in board meetings to demonstrate support of clients.
• Tracked individual agency sales to monitor use of program.

CLIENT RELATIONS

Established a reputation for highly reliable and personalized service to clients of SPACE & LEISURE Travel Consortium:
• Trained agency staff on how to use the supplier program.
• Taught owners to maximize profits thru exclusive utilization of our program.
• Called on agencies monthly to service their accounts:
-Developed and maintained a friendly personal relationship with each agency.
-Served as liaison to quickly resolve agencies' problems with program suppliers.

EMPLOYMENT HISTORY

1986-88	**Regional Sales Manager**	SPACE & LEISURE Travel Consortium, Pompano Beach FL
1985-86	**Sales Manager & PR**	SPACE & LEISURE Travel Consortium for Consortium's NEWPORT BEACH HOTEL, Miami Beach FL
1984-85	**PR & Business Manager**	FREDDIE SOLOMON CORP., professional athlete
1982-83	**PR & Business Manager**	DWIGHT CLARK, professional athlete
1979-84	**Account Officer***	BANK OF AMERICA, Redwood City CA
	*concurrent with PR positions above	
1974-79	**Customer Service Rep**	DANA CORP., automotive, Manteca CA

FRED SANDERS

1029 Lincoln Ave.
San Francisco CA 94110
(415) 995-3803

Objective: Position as General Manager/CEO,
providing leadership and direction for **business development** by
increasing market share/profitability, and reducing risk and loss.

HIGHLIGHTS OF QUALIFICATIONS

★ Over 25 years practical, broad-based management experience, with a
realistic understanding of market constraints and opportunities.

★ Track record of responsibility for managing complex projects
involving thousands of customers, with millions of dollars of investment.

★ Conceptual talent for seeing 'the big picture,' pinpointing an organizational
objective, and setting goals and priorities to achieve it.

★ Adept in applying marketing theory to successful business development.

RELEVANT EXPERIENCE & ACCOMPLISHMENTS

BUSINESS DEVELOPMENT

· In 25 years as entreprenurial CEO, helped organizations consistently grow in
sales, profits, returns, safety, and acceptance, by expanding and strengthening
through: -product development -system enhancement -financial controls
-merger -affiliation -marketing and sales.

MARKETING MANAGEMENT

· Developed a highly effective customer-oriented **product evaluation process**
featuring direct customer feedback and trade association market research.
Created marketing plans, incorporating 8-10 of the most appropriate media,
scheduled by a PERT method and budgeted in accordance with expected returns.

· Developed valuable **professional rapport with regulating agencies**, and set
standards for product development, marketplace acceptance, advertising and
promotion, sales and product delivery, customer relations.

OPERATIONS & PERSONNEL

· **Developed operations systems** integrated with production and marketing,
greatly improving profitability.

· **Built a strong team** of front-line managers with excellent esprit de corps, by
implementing regular management meetings, improved training, and incentives.

· Developed a **highly effective management system** for efficiently processing a
high volume of prospective customers through a multi-step sales process.

FINANCE; RISK ASSESSMENT

· **Established initial financial plan and forecast** for several large projects which
are still in effect 7 or more years later.

· Successfully developed FIRST EQUITY from under $1 million in gross receipts to
over $12 million, with internally generated funds.

- **Continued on page two** -

RELEVANT EXPERIENCE & ACCOMPLISHMENTS
(continued)

ADMINISTRATION; LITIGATION
· **Created a management information system** that provided, for the first time, the activity of each operational component, making it possible to accurately forecast product development.
· **Adapted** a multiple-department **management system** to successfully administer more than 50 funds concurrently.
· Developed an **expertise in loss prevention management** through experience coordinating and assessing approximately 100 potential lawsuits; 75% settled without litigation.

EMPLOYMENT HISTORY

1987-present **Chairman**
(general contracting firm since 1972, specializing in manufacturing, building, remodeling, and maintenance of equipment)
ALLIED INDUSTRIES, Sacramento

1986-present **Consultant**
(real estate consulting for the lending and mortgage insurance industry)
INTEGRATED ASSETS, San Francisco

1973-85 **President**
(real estate development)
FIRST EQUITY INC., San Francisco

1972-73 **Vice President**
(real estate management)
GENERAL PROPERTIES, INC., San Jose

1969-72 **Director of Administration**
(real estate and hotel development)
AMERA CORP., San Francisco

EDUCATION
B.A., Public Administration
University of Maryland

Fred thoroughly breaks down the functions of a CEO/manager, and then documents his accomplishments in each area.

MELANIE A. GARAMONDI

5775 Skyline Way
Mill Valley CA 94965
(415) 909-6889

Objective: Position as Staff Accountant

HIGHLIGHTS OF QUALIFICATIONS

★ 7 years experience in bookkeeping, through financial statements, in a wide range of industries.
★ Completed CPA exam, November 1987.
★ 3.85 cumulative GPA at Golden Gate University; currently enrolled in Masters Program in Tax.
★ Licensed California Real Estate Broker.
★ Strength in recognizing, analyzing and solving problems.

PROFESSIONAL EXPERIENCE

TAX PLANNING
• Developed and implemented **start-up financial systems** for various businesses (law, real estate, property management, construction, landscape contracting, physician) to assure **compliance with tax law and identify allowable tax benefits.**

BUSINESS ORGANIZATION
• **Designed customized business plans and financial systems** for single proprietorships, professional corporations, real estate partnerships, and a nonprofit corporation.

TROUBLE-SHOOTING
• **Successfully clarified the financial status** of a nonprofit experiencing financial chaos:
  - Confirmed the financial statements for the previous 3 years.
  - Designed a simpler and more comprehensive record-keeping system.
  - Created a new budget.
  - Performed audit with CPAs.

COMPUTER CONVERSION
• Conducted a **computer conversion** for a property management company and 5 partnerships each owning a shopping center:
  - Selected and helped debug the software.
  - Traced flow of documents and revised collection of documentary evidence.
  - Hired and collaborated with tax accountant to improve tax planning.
  - Rewrote leases for maximum clarity and legal benefits for lessor.
  - Prepared budgets for capital projects and monitored actual costs.

CLIENT REP/ADVISOR
• Served as **financial advisor** to business clients:
  - Represented owners and management at business meetings and conferences, as their specialist in real estate and financial matters.
  - Appraised management of financial trends and implications of changes in tax law and GAAP.

EMPLOYMENT HISTORY

1988-present	Student and travel	Golden Gate University, San Francisco
1987 fall	**Accountant**	Legal Aid of Rowland Heights
1985-87	**Bookkeeper**	Carghill Property Management, San Francisco
1981-85	**Bookkeeper**	Independent; clients in law, real estate, construction.
1976-81	**Real Estate Agent/Broker**	Millhurst and Granger, Marin County

EDUCATION

CPA courses 1982-86 • Currently enrolled/MS, Tax • GOLDEN GATE UNIVERSITY
B.A., English - UNIVERSITY OF CALIFORNIA, BERKELEY

BROOK BARNUM

6000 MacArthur Blvd., Apt. 3
Oakland CA 94605
(415) 909-6666

Objective: New position with Ten Speed Press as Assistant to Warehouse Manager/Liaison between Warehouse & Management

SUMMARY

★ 7 years experience with Ten Speed; record of loyalty and dependability.
★ Hard working, ambitious, willing to learn.
★ Able to view problems in a positive way, and propose solutions to streamline operations and improve working conditions.
★ Excellent working relations with warehouse staff; skill and experience as liaison between warehouse and office.

PROPOSALS FOR IMPROVEMENT

ASSISTING MANAGEMENT

- Establish uniform quantity of books-per-box, allowing for:
  -efficient stacking and shipping
  -more accurate inventory
  -eliminating damage to books.
- Establish uniform labeling of boxes from printer.
- Install computer terminal at warehouse for immediate update of inventory.

COMMUNICATION / LIAISON

- Hold monthly meetings of warehouse management and office management to:
  -keep warehouse staff fully informed about new titles
  -anticipate and prepare for changes in workload
  -maintain fullest communication between warehouse and management
  -update warehouse staff on changes in office personnel and job responsibilities
  -discuss shipping and packing problems and develop solutions.
- Hold quarterly meetings of all company personnel to improve morale and provide opportunity for staff to present problems for discussion.
- Involve warehouse staff in interviewing and hiring process to assure that new employees have adequate experience, valid driving license, and good work attitude.

EMPLOYMENT HISTORY

1983-present	**Assistant Foreman**	Warehouse, TEN SPEED PRESS
1981-83	**Warehouseman**	Warehouse, TEN SPEED PRESS
1980-81	**Assistant Foreman**	ON-LINE MICROCENTERS, Hayward
1979-80	**Co-Owner/Gardener**	NATURAL GARDENER, Oakland

EDUCATION

Chabot College, 1980

VIVIAN MARIE BARLOW
45998 Martin Luther King Jr. Way,
Berkeley CA 94703
(415) 789-2221 home

Objective: Marketing/Promotions with a manufacturer of quality clothing
involving •Image development •Community relations
•Special events coordination and/or •Product development.

HIGHLIGHTS OF QUALIFICATIONS

★ BFA in Fashion Merchandising and Retail Management.

★ Sure, intuitive sense for products destined to succeed.

★ Experience in image development, special events coordination, and national advertising campaigns for major recording artists.

★ Proven ability to capture a new market, through unique and creative marketing concepts.

★ Skill in developing a powerful business network.

★ Able to represent a company with professionalism and confidence.

RELEVANT SKILLS & ACCOMPLISHMENTS

MARKET DEVELOPMENT

• **Managed the start-up** of a successful new company, DATA SERVICES:
  -Identified the initial target market, maximizing usefulness of existing contacts.
  -Established a business base in local government as a springboard, successfully expanding to the Midwest and West Coast, thus generating $18 million in sales since start-up.

PRODUCT DESIGN, DEVELOPMENT, ACCEPTANCE

• **Collaborated** in high-tech **product design** as VP Marketing at DATA SERVICES:
  -**Assessed** local government's most pressing **problems** (i.e., need for revenue, more efficient local services, overcrowding of prisons, etc.).
  -**Developed** model **products** to address these issues (software to process parking tickets and water bills; 911 computer-aided-dispatch systems for police cars; inmate tracking and resource allocation systems).

COMMUNITY RELATIONS/PUBLIC RELATIONS

• Developed an **extensive network** of business relationships throughout the US. Currently active in 5 influential national organizations and numerous local organizations.
• Enhanced the **public image** of DATA SERVICES by contributing an educational and entertaining event (demo of multipurpose robot) for local school districts.
• Served as **spokesperson** for DATA SERVICES within the community, appearing on public panels and participating in workshops on public affairs.

- Continued on page 2 -

Vivian wants to get back to her "first love," fashion merchandising. She livens up her resume with enough detail (see Special Events Coordination) to capture the reader's interest.

RELEVANT SKILLS & ACCOMPLISHMENTS, continued

SPECIAL EVENTS COORDINATION

- As Dir. of Marketing for a national concert promotion firm, Trivera & Co.:
  -Developed and implemented **concepts for a national advertising campaign**.
  -Arranged **special promotion** events: coordinated all logistics for in-store promotions; arranged radio/TV/print interviews for featured recording artists.
  -Conducted **study of market factors** to plan tour schedule and route.
  -Elicited support of record companies and **cooperative sponsorship** of major beverage companies to offset tour costs.

- **Managed fund-raising activities**, for example:
  -"All This Jam For Your Bread," LaBelle concert on Halloween for New York City mayoral candidate.
  -Thanksgiving food drives and Christmas toy drives, bringing major recording artists to local communities.

- As Account Executive for Barberry Advertising, the company handling the state lottery account:
  -**Coordinated** the first Grand Prize Drawing, featuring local celebrities.
  -**Originated** the first "Losers' Drawing," featuring a well-known TV personality using a cement mixer as the tumbler from which to draw the tickets.

EMPLOYMENT HISTORY

1984-present	**VP Marketing**	DATA SERVICES INC., New York NY (consultants in automated data processing)
1983-84	**Executive Asst. to CEO**	AEROCOMP INC., New York NY (aerospace and defense computer systems)
1982-83	**Account Executive**	BARBERRY ADVERTISING, New York NY (lottery advertising agency)
1979-82	**Director of Advertising**	TRIVERA & CO. (national concert promotion company)

EDUCATION

B.F.A., Fashion Merchandising, Retail Management, Summa cum laude
FASHION INSTITUTE OF TECHNOLOGY, New York City, 1976
Graduate Studies, Computer Science, 1985 - HOWARD UNIVERSITY, Washington DC

PROFESSIONAL NETWORK

National Conference of Black Mayors
National Forum for Black Public Administrators
National Association of County Officials
American Management Association
Public Technology Inc.

LORRAINE CHAPMAN

7855 West End Avenue
Lafayette CA 94549
(415) 999-8745

Just out of college a year, and without much work experience, Lorraine explores the possibilities in entry level public policy work. She chose a CHRONOLOGICAL FORMAT yet still emphasized the experience most relevant to her tentative goal.

Objective: **Position as a research assistant, legislative advocate, and/or press aide with a public policy organization.**

Highlights of Qualifications

★ Strong communication and research skills.
★ Successful in promoting an organization and generating funding.
★ Willing and able to handle a wide variety of tasks.
★ Creative, resourceful, and thorough in developing a project.

EMPLOYMENT / RELEVANT EXPERIENCE

1987 *Administrative Asst.* – MATT KURLE INC., IMPORTER/DISTRIBUTOR, Orinda CA

Jan-Aug 1987 *Current Affairs Research Intern* – KQED PUBLIC TV, San Francisco CA

COMMUNICATION & RESEARCH SKILLS

- **Investigated program topics** for "Express" show and "MacNeil/Lehrer Newshour" involving extensive library research and interviewing.
- **Negotiated with government and private agencies** for data and film footage.
- Summarized research and **prepared informational packets** for producers.
- **Pre-interviewed** studio guests. **Wrote position papers** for show moderator.

1985-86 *Assistant Director* – ASUCD STUDENT FORUMS, University of California, Davis

PROGRAM DEVELOPMENT - MEDIA/PUBLICITY

- **Collaborated on the planning, promotion,** and production of 30 public lectures (total audience 32,000). Speakers included Geraldine Ferraro, author Alice Walker, physicist Edward Teller.
  - **Corresponded** with prospective speakers and scheduled appearance dates.
  - **Organized event logistics:** seating, security, decor.
  - **Coordinated and scheduled publicity;** prepared advertising budget.
- **Conceived and produced a comprehensive TV program** on AIDS which was tied in with community AIDS Awareness Week.
  - **Won funding** of $2,000 for the project through written and oral presentations.
  - **Wrote press releases,** PSAs, advertising copy; worked with graphic artists on design of promotional materials.
  - **Secured media coverage** and re-broadcasting of the event on community TV.
  - Earned commendations from university administration and City of Davis.

FUND-RAISING - COMMUNITY RELATIONS

- **Successfully won support and funding** from campus and civic organizations through a variety of means:
  - **Met with organizational directors** to present program ideas and needs, securing donations of services: catering, limousine services, publicity.
  - **Coordinated and promoted fund-raising receptions** attended by civic leaders, generating significant funds for ASUCD and broad media coverage.

EDUCATION

B.A. Economics, cum laude, University of California, Davis 1986
Education Abroad Program - Tokyo, Japan, Summer 1986

ESTELLE GADE

9843 Thirty-second Ave.
Oakland CA 94605
(415) 614-2020

Estelle is fairly new in the work force. She uses a chronological format but still emphasizes the experience most important to her new job. Notice how she presents in-school jobs. Estelle's cover letter is on page 61.

Objective: Banking customer service position.

Highlights of Qualifications

★ Experience helping customers and solving problems.
★ Good with figures and record keeping, using CRT.
★ Hard worker who does more than is expected.
★ Successfully cleaned up a 2-year backlog of claims.
★ Enjoy keeping busy, learning new skills, and developing
   systems to get the job done better and faster.

RELATED WORK EXPERIENCE

Nov'87–present   **Customer Service Rep,   UNION CENTRAL BANK,** Oakland
• Advised customers on banking products: loans, Bankcards, investment services.
• Assisted customers in cashing checks, making deposits and loan payments.
• Answered phones; referred customers to other bank employees for various
  services.
• Balanced figures for total daily transactions.

Jan'87–June'87   **Claims Processor,   MAPLEHURST MEDICAL GROUP,** Oakland
• Cleaned up a major back-log of medical payment claims from local hospitals:
  -handled approximately 500 claims/week, at least double the amount expected
  -paid drug claims, processing for payment over 100 claims/day
  -found duplicate bills and duplicate payments
  -filled out benefit computation sheets, using specific codes to identify
   physicians,vendors, and patients
  -answered calls from irate customers, assuring them of prompt service.
• Handled incoming calls from patients:
  -processed health plan membership applications
  -helped patients choose their primary care physician
  -approved reimbursement payments for out-of-pocket expenses.
• Used CRT daily to enter payments on patients' records (adding correct codes
  for medical services) and to verify status of incoming claims for payment.

Nov'86–Dec'86   **Sales/Customer Service,   SEE'S CANDIES,** Hayward
• Provided good quality customer service for high volume of Christmas shoppers.
• Helped employers select bulk purchases as holiday gifts for their employees.

Summer 1986   **Office Assistant, DAMN GOOD RESUME SERVICE,** Berkeley
• Contacted hundreds of clients by phone and letter, getting permissions to
  use materials in a book to be published. Kept detailed records of contacts.

Additional Work History
Part-time jobs during high school

Nov'84–Apr'85	**Bookkeeper**	**MacDONALD'S,** Oakland
Oct'83–Nov'84	**Cashier**	**MacDONALD's,** Oakland & Hayward
Summer '83	**Clerk**	**HAVENSCOURT COMMUNITY CHURCH,** Oakland

EDUCATION & TRAINING
CHABOT COLLEGE, one semester, Business Administration
Data entry experience on IBM and NCR computers

LESLIE M. GOSS

3001 Acacia Drive
San Francisco CA 94114
(415) 133-7889

Objective: Administrative management position, with a focus on special projects, program management, and community relations.

Highlights of Qualifications

★ Competent, reliable, and committed professional, with a proven record of success in assuming increasing levels of responsibility.

★ Outstanding organizational skills, with a talent for "seeing the big picture."

★ Strength in management of special projects and creative program design.

★ Skills in research, analysis and administrative problem solving.

★ Articulate and persuasive in written and verbal presentations.

PROFESSIONAL EXPERIENCE

ADMINISTRATION / MANAGEMENT

As entrepreneur

• Created and managed a successful business, offering meeting planning services:
  - Wrote a business plan: defined goals and developed cash flow/break-even analysis.
  - Designed promotional materials and marketed the business.
  - Built a substantial client base; sold the business as a profitable venture.

• Developed administrative systems to manage special projects, including computerized records management.

• Produced and implemented marketing and public relations plans for special projects.

As staff member

• As Executive Assistant to administration department of the Rural Alaska Community Action Program:
  - Supervised administrative support staff (2 employees).
  - Served as staff liaison to a 21-member board of directors.
    ...prepared all reports to directors   ...maintained corporate records
    ...filed corporate resolutions with legislative committees.

• Supervised a 7-person research group, and developed a proposal which succeeded in establishing initial $250,000 funding for Alaska Consumer Advocacy Program.

PROGRAM DEVELOPMENT / SPECIAL PROJECTS

• Managed several large conferences and special projects each year, as owner and manager of The Coordinators meeting planning firm.
  Typical Project, a major annual conference on Early Childhood Education:
  - Developed the program, in collaboration with sponsor's advisory committee.
  - Introduced the use of key national speakers.
  - Developed corporate sponsorships and targeted marketing.
  - Over 4-year period, built attendance from 300 to 800 participants, and transformed the conference into a profit-making event.

• Established a unique new program, The Internship Program for Alaska, providing intern staffing to a wide range of nonprofit organizations:
  - Authored a successful grant proposal, including definition of program content.
  - Hired and guided the first director in initial implementation of the program.

• Authored and published:
    ...newsletters ...brochures ...conference proceedings ...numerous proposals.

- Continued on Page Two -

Leslie's resume makes extensive use of the "Compound One-Liner" format. Her goal is to make a transition to the for-profit sector.

PROFESSIONAL EXPERIENCE
(continued)

COMMUNITY RELATIONS
- Successfully acquired corporate sponsorship for conferences and special projects.
- Developed a photographic study of a neighborhood, which illustrated the need for rehabilitation services, and was effective in gaining funding for the program.
- Served by appointment of the Mayor of Anchorage, on a Task Force charged with equitable allocation funding for social services agencies, involving negotiation and teamwork.

EMPLOYMENT HISTORY

1987-88	**Meetings Manager**	THE HEALTHCARE FORUM, San Francisco
		(formerly The Association of Western Hospitals)
1983-87	**Manager/Owner**	THE COORDINATORS (meeting planning firm), Anchorage
1981-83	**Executive Asst.**	RURAL ALASKA COMMUNITY ACTION PROGRAM
1980-81	**Executive Director**	ALASKA PUBLIC INTEREST RESEARCH GROUP
1978-80	**Deputy Director**	ALASKA PUBLIC INTEREST RESEARCH GROUP
1977-78	**Administrative Asst.**	VISUAL ARTS CENTER, Anchorage
1975-77	**Continuity Director**	NORTHERN TELEVISION, INC., KTVA-TV, Anchorage

EDUCATION

B.A., Creative Arts - SAN FRANCISCO STATE UNIVERSITY, 1974

Portfolio of projects available for review.
References available on request.

DIRECTOR OF OFFICE OPERATIONS

JOHN J. REED
421 Jasper Alley
San Francisco CA 94133
(415) 937-0099

A waiter for 20 years, John aims for a major care change, back to an earlier interest in electronics He'll use this DRAFT RESUME for some INFOR-MATIONAL INTERVIEWING (see page 23) to ex-plore how he could gain entry into the field and apply his experience and training from 20 years ago.

Objective: Entry level position as electronics engineering technician, involving field service and/or research and development.

HIGHLIGHTS OF QUALIFICATIONS

★ Very strong commitment to developing a career in electronics.
★ Productive and responsible; willing to learn and handle any tasks needed.
★ Skill in tracing schematic diagrams, analyzing circuits, trouble-shooting problems.
    -Heald College training as Electronics Engineering Technician.
    -Two years as Army radio mechanic and instructor in radio repair.
★ Over 20 years experience in successfully dealing with customers.
★ Able to represent a company with a professional appearance and manner.

RELEVANT SKILLS & EXPERIENCE

Electronics Knowledge
- Completed 2-year course at Heald College, in Electronics Engineering Technology.
- Completed math, physics, and drafting courses at City College:
  -Algebra -Geometry -Trigonometry -Calculus -Physics -Drafting
- Taught radio repair in US Army Signal Corps.
- **Rebuilt and rewired** electrical home appliances.
- **Replaced portion of house wiring**, bringing it up to code.

Trouble-Shooting/Research
- **Researched** in technical manuals and consulted with professionals in the field, to resolve technical problems in home/auto repair; experience in use of hand tools in wood-working and metal-working.
- **Diagnosed problems** in home electronics: TVs, radios, disc players, tape decks.

Customer Relations
- Developed a successful, professional approach to providing **top quality customer service**, consistently applying these principles:
  -Create atmosphere that encourages the customer to freely express complaints.
  -Thoroughly and tactfully research the potential solutions to their problem.
  -Get feedback to be sure the customer is, in fact, satisfied with the results.

EMPLOYMENT HISTORY

1968-present	**Waiter**	ROHDALE'S RESTAURANT, San Francisco
1983-87	**Consultant** to Restaurant Management	
	Part-time (concurrent with above); advising management on personnel problems and professional standards in restaurant service.	
1966-68	**Field Radio Repairman & Instructor**	U.S. ARMY SIGNAL CORP

EDUCATION & TRAINING
Graduate, HEALD COLLEGE, Electronics Engineering Technician
US ARMY, Field Radio Repair

WILLIAM P. MAJOUÉ
P.O. Box 83
Point Reyes Station CA 94956
(415) 404-0900

Bill wrote this resume for INFORMATIONAL IN-TERVIEWING (see page 23). He loves bikes and is exploring the possibility of working for a bike manufacturer using the expertise he gained selling top quality bicycles. Bill's cover letter appears on page 59.

Objective: Position with a manufacturer of quality bike components, involving:
•marketing support •field liaison •aid in research and development.

SUMMARY OF QUALIFICATIONS

★ 2-1/2 years experience in assembling and retailing top quality bikes, serving as store assistant manager, and overseeing service department.
★ Ability to recognize functional and marketable component designs and recommend them for possible rights purchase.
★ High level of creative energy, combined with strong organizational skills.
★ Effective communication liaison between builder/designer and manufacturer.

RELEVANT EXPERIENCE

As Shop Manager and Service Manager for Point Reyes Bikes...

Made **design recommendations to builder/designers:**
• Provided feedback on how their designs were received by customers.
• Advised them on newest components available.
• Assessed designs for efficiency of operation.
• Experimented with the integration of different components of various manufacturers.

Developed reputation of respect among customers and builders for **expert product knowledge**, honesty, and customer service with a personal touch:
• Interpreted to the customer the designer's unique approach and its advantages and disadvantages.
• Advised customers on specific components and after-market products, for durability and how they function under various conditions.
• Assessed customers' wants and needs and made realistic recommendations based on actual projected use.

EMPLOYMENT HISTORY

1988-present	**Shop/Service Manager**	POINT REYES BIKES, Point Reyes CA
1987	**Electrician**	SELF EMPLOYED & CONTRACT WORK
1985-86	**Mail Order/Shipping**	POINT REYES BIKES, Point Reyes CA
1980-84	**Electrician/Solar Installer**	SELF EMPLOYED & CONTRACT WORK
1978-79	**Electrician/Plumber**	HOME REPAIR SERVICE, San Rafael CA

EDUCATION & TRAINING
Electrical Engineering, DELGADO JR. COLLEGE, New Orleans LA
Brooks Institute of Photography, Santa Barbara CA

RUBEN E. LOPEZ

515 John Muir Drive, San Francisco CA 94123
(415) 909-5755 home • (415) 809-1000 office

Objective: Position as High School Principal

EDUCATION

M.A., **School Administration**, UNIVERSITY OF THE PACIFIC, Stockton CA
B.A., History and Physical Education, UNIVERSITY OF THE PACIFIC

Lifetime **Teaching Credentials**: General Elementary and Secondary
Lifetime **Administrative Credentials**: Standard, Elementary, and Secondary

PROFESSIONAL AFFILIATIONS

Association of California School Administrators
United Administrators of San Francisco

HIGHLIGHTS OF QUALIFICATIONS

★ 19-year background in administration, at State Department of Education, high school, and university levels.

★ Experience in all aspects of high school operations: curriculum development, academic department head, dean of students, personnel evaluation, master schedule building.

★ Effective principal of a large comprehensive high school (ADA 2300), comprising a very diverse ethnic population.

★ A creative and "take-charge" type administrator;
proven ability to see what needs to be done, and do it.

PROFESSIONAL EXPERIENCE & ACCOMPLISHMENTS

Assistant Principal	BALBOA HIGH SCHOOL, San Francisco CA
1985-present	MISSION HIGH SCHOOL, San Francisco CA

· Developed a **successful plan for dropout prevention** featuring one-on-one instruction for truant and high-risk students. **Results**:
-eliminated disruptive classroom behavior; -reduced after school detention;
-upgraded the educational atmosphere;   -increased revenues for ADA.

· **Recovered over $200,000 in ADA revenues** for the school district:
-restructured work schedule of the attendance technician to provide needed time and facilities for documenting legitimate absences.

1983-85 **Management Intern** AMFAC CORP., Food Division, Morgan Hill CA

· Trained staff and developed personnel for middle management positions.

1981-83 **Director,** Special Projects UNION SCHOOL DIST., Sacramento CA

· Oversaw implementation and evaluation of federal and state special projects and programs for the District.

- Continued on Page two -

RUBEN E. LOPEZ
Page two

Ruben's resume shows how you can focus on your unique achievements rather than job descriptions even when using a CHRONOLOGICAL FORMAT Ruben's cover letter is on page 60.

PROFESSIONAL EXPERIENCE & ACCOMPLISHMENTS
(continued)

1978-81   **Principal**   UNION HIGH SCHOOL, Sacramento CA

- Initiated the **updating of course descriptions and expansion of course offerings**, to accommodate the needs of both low achievers and gifted students.
- **Originated** and coordinated a highly successful "**Career Day**" program, which:
  -provided students an in-depth exposure to a wide range of occupations;
  -helped teachers to relate their subject matter to the world of work.
- **Spearheaded a successful fund-raising drive** to replace antiquated lighting for school football field, raising $30,000 through a specially arranged carnival.
  Coordinated the joint efforts of parents, students, community business leaders, and city officials to support this project.
- **Increased ADA revenues** by $45,000 by initiating an in-school study hall program which tremendously reduced class-cutting.
- Effectively **reduced youth gang activity on campus** by bringing together a task force of parents and community representatives, including state legislators and local law enforcement agencies.
- **Initiated** the formation of a **minority student club** to increase participation in campus activities. **Results:**
  -raised self-esteem and enhanced image with other students;
  -elected the first Hispanic female student body president;
  -developed a stabilizing force for working with youth gangs;
  -involved minority student in sponsorship of a popular annual talent show.
- **Chaired meetings** for the **highly sensitive process** of re-leagueing 30 high schools of the Southern Conference/Central Coast Section, collaborating with 30 high school principals and athletic directors.
  Won recognition for providing **outstanding and effective leadership**.

1976-78 **Asst. Principal,** Curriculum   EVERETT HIGH SCHOOL, Salinas CA

- Developed and coordinated **Master Schedule**.
- Chaired the District's Student Attendance Review Board.
- Represented my high school on District Professional Curriculum Committee.

1972-76 **Educational Consultant** STATE DEPT. OF EDUCATION, Sacramento

- Led instructional team in the **development and review of curriculum** for educationally disadvantaged students statewide.
- Oversaw disbursement of $18.3 million for compensatory education programs statewide.

1969-72 **Project Director**   UNIVERSITY OF THE PACIFIC, Stockton CA

- Coordinated and developed a pilot program funded by the federal government which entailed development of a GED curriculum for high school dropouts; recruited and placed students into college, job training programs, and jobs.

PIETRO (PETER) CARNINI

341 San Jose Boulevard
San Francisco CA 94102
(415) 098-4333

Objective: Position as waiter in a top quality restaurant.

SUMMARY OF QUALIFICATIONS

★ Over 6 years experience as a professional waiter.
★ Demonstrated record of exceptional reliability.
★ Able to think independently and quickly resolve problems.
★ Expertise in anticipating and responding to customer needs.
★ Sophisticated knowledge of wines and liquors.
★ Take pride in providing excellent customer service.

RELEVANT SKILLS & EXPERIENCE

CUSTOMER RELATIONS

• Developed an effective approach for advising customers on food and wine, e.g.:
   -listening for customers' likes/dislikes, to make appropriate suggestions
   -using appealing, descriptive phrases to describe dishes
   -recommending wines that complement specific entrees
   -sensing and responding to the moods and needs of each customer.
• Fostered repeat customers through consistently providing quick, well-timed, and professional service.

TEAMWORK / PROBLEM SOLVING

• With 6 years experience, developed a strategy for making quick decisions under high stress conditions, maintaining composure while prioritizing and orchestrating the many job functions.
• Built an exceptional record of reliability...3 years without a missed day.
• Earned a reputation as a valuable and cooperative co-worker, by:
   -being fair, honest, and willing to help others when needed
   -effectively resolving conflicts at appropriate times
   -assisting new managers and other staff to become familiar with restaurant policy and operations.

EMPLOYMENT HISTORY

1985-88	**Dinner Waiter**	REX SOLE'S RESTAURANT, Berkeley CA
1983-85	**Lunch/Dinner Waiter**	CARDINAL'S HOUSE RESTAURANT, Portland OR
1980-83	**Dinner Waiter**	MAZZIE'S RESTAURANT, Salem OR
1980-82	**Assistant Manager**	WALDEN BOOKS, Salem OR

EDUCATION

History Major, 1977-80 - WILLAMETTE UNIVERSITY, Salem OR

JOSEPHINE TRICKLER

1408 Wisteria Blvd.
Berkeley CA 94705
(415) 699-8771

Objective: Position as Supermarket Checker or Head Clerk

SUMMARY OF QUALIFICATIONS

★ 16 years experience in the grocery industry, as head clerk, checker, and cashier.

★ Excellent reputation with customers as a competent, knowledgeable and helpful professional.

★ Enjoy my work and consistently greet customers with a smile.

★ Honest, reliable, and productive.

RELEVANT SKILLS & EXPERIENCE

CUSTOMER SERVICE

- Developed a reputation for **excellent customer service** by:
  -acknowledging the customer's presence and making eye contact.
  -greeting customers in a friendly manner, and giving them full attention.
  -taking time to answer a question or find someone else who could.

- Served as **product expert** on sophisticated items, directing customers to:
  -exotic spices and ingredients -ethnic foods -unusual gourmet items.

- **Increased sales** in the higher profit Natural Foods Department (and increased customer satisfaction) by **advising customers** on bulk alternatives to name-brand items.

SUPERVISION

- As Head Clerk, **managed "front end"** of the store:
  -**prepared daily schedules** for staff of up to 18 clerks, to assure maximum checkstand coverage at all times.
  -**assigned staff** to cover peak hours and continuous stocking.

- **Trained** new clerks.

ADMINISTRATIVE

- **Balanced** checker's **cash drawer** with consistently high level of accuracy.

- As **Office Cashier** for one year:
  -accurately balanced books and balanced deposits
  -answered phones -prepared daily sales report -made deposits
  -processed returned checks -prepared monthly sales report for HQ.

EMPLOYMENT HISTORY

1970-present	**Retail Clerk**, journeyman	COOP SUPERMARKET, Berkeley CA and MAYFAIR MARKET, Oakland CA (bought by COOP in 1974)
1970	**Buyer's Assistant**	CAPWELL'S, Oakland
1965-70	**Manager's Assistant**	RUSANN'S Clothing Store, Spokane WA

EDUCATION

Business Classes, 1969 - SPOKANE COMMUNITY COLLEGE

MARIA DOSHAN
4408 Cedar Lake Road • Santa Rosa, California 95401 • (408) 888-6754

Objective: Position as **Health Plan Marketing Trainer.**

Committed to the educational process, guiding students to achieve
mastery of skills and realization of their own goals and objectives.

HIGHLIGHTS OF QUALIFICATIONS

★ 7 years professional experience in seminar design and delivery,
including facilitation of an employee training program.

★ Keen intuition; warm, sincere, down-to-earth teaching style.

★ Special talent for creating an environment conducive to learning.

★ Effective team member who is comfortable with leading or collaborating.

★ 10 years experience in successful health care marketing.

REPRESENTATIVE SKILLS & ACCOMPLISHMENTS

PROGRAM DEVELOPMENT & PRESENTATION

• Designed and presented **seminars** for hospital middle-managers on the effective
use of various management reports:
-**developed learning materials** (handbooks, exercises, reading lists, audio-visuals,
evaluation forms)
-assisted managers in increasing department productivity and cost efficiency.

• **Developed** and delivered group **presentations at national, regional, and local**
conferences for health care professionals, on productivity measurement.

• **Presented an overview on marketing** to senior employees for Education and
Training Department's "Reorientation" program.

TRAINING

• **Created and conducted** on-going quarterly **training programs** for nonprofessional
health care staff, consistent with Medicare standards for home care.

• **Trained** nurses, respiratory therapists, and pharmacists on appropriate use of
pharmaceutical products.

• Chosen as participant **trainer at four annual sales conferences**, to share successful
sales strategies with colleagues.

• **Performed and taught** creative dramatics;
trained educators on the use of creative dramatics in the classroom.

SALES & MARKETING EXPERTISE

• Earned **sales achievement award** for 3 consecutive years:
-produced largest single sale of new clients from a multi-hospital system;
-retained client base without loss, for 2 years (the only representative to
accomplish this).

• Delivered **highly successful sales presentations** to employer groups, outlining
Kaiser benefit package, and contributing to a major membership increase (+2400).

• Researched and presented a **marketing assessment** for Kaiser Medical Center, well
received by joint administrative team and department chiefs.

- Employment History and Education on Page two -

MARIA DOSHAN
Page two

Maria got feedback from the employer that her resume was one of the best among 40 applications for the job. Maria's cover letter is on page 60.

EMPLOYMENT HISTORY

1987-present	**Health Plan Representative**	KAISER PERMANENTE
1982-86	**Sales Consultant**	AMERICAN HOSPITAL ASSOC., Chicago IL
1981-82	**Marketing Director**	MEDICAL HOME CARE, Chicago IL
1979-81	**Sales Representative**	DORSEY LABORATORIES, Chicago IL
1978-79	**Sales Representative**	TEXAS PHARMACAL, Chicago IL
1978	**Supervisor**	KELLY SERVICES, Chicago IL Interviewed and tested job applicants.
1976-78	**Instructor, Dramatics**	CLIMB, INC., Chicago IL

EDUCATION & PROFESSIONAL DEVELOPMENT

B.A., with honors, **Education/Theatre Arts** - UNIVERSITY OF CHICAGO, 1976

•Time Management Seminar 1988   •Persuasive Selling Skills 1984/1987   •Negotiation Skills 1988

ROBERT VENTURI
5726 Solano Ave.
Richmond CA 94805
(415) 236-1077

Objective: Position as Park Supervisor with regional park district.

Highlights of Qualifications

★ Over 25 years professional experience in horticulture, developing excellent knowledge of landscaping and plants.
★ Lifelong interest and background in gardening.
★ Excellent working relations with the public, and with co-workers and employees of all ethnic groups.
★ Proven record of reliability and responsibility.
★ Skill in planning, coordinating and supervising projects.

RELEVANT EXPERIENCE

SUPERVISION, TRAINING, SAFETY

• As Landscape Maintenance Supervisor at Systek:
  -**supervised and scheduled** 35 permanent gardeners and 6 foremen
  -**trained and evaluated** the above employees, teaching:
     ...safe use of power tools ...principles of horticulture ...chemical pest control.

• **Supervised** 20-40 CETA gardeners, both youth and adults:
  -presented **safety guidelines** at mandatory weekly safety meetings
  -followed-up and **monitored attendance** and **productivity**
  -**taught** proper use of equipment and tools
  -**taught** pruning techniques, weed control, turf management
  -organized and planned field trips to botanical sites.

• **Trained and supervised** hundreds of seasonal gardening helpers, students at UC Berkeley working at Botanical Gardens.
• CPR and First Aid Certificate.

PARK TECHNICAL EXPERIENCE

• Operated all **equipment and power tools**:
     ...walk mowers ...riding mowers ...gas and electric trimmers ...lawn edgers
     ...lawn vacuums ...generators ...rotary reel and gang mowers ...tractors
     ...turf equipment and attachments ...chain saws ...weed eaters ...brush cutters.

• **Maintained** grounds and greenhouses at UCB Botanical gardens, involving:
     ...small engine repair ...concrete construction ...paving
     ...repair of patios/driveways/foundations ...greenhouse construction ...excavating
     ...grading (residential, commercial) ...industrial lot cleaning ...tree removal
     ...slide repair ...erosion control ...plumbing ...drain cleaning
     ...sprinkler system installation   ...maintenance of athletic fields
     ...fertilization ...chemical applications (weed control) ...rototilling ...sod lawns
     ...pest control ...irrigating ...planting ...mowing lawns ...pruning ...special soil mixing.

• Maintained school district truck; excellent driving record.
• Maintained indoor plants at Systek offices and school administration offices.

- Continued on page two -

ROBERT VENTURI
page two

RELEVANT EXPERIENCE (continued)

ADMINISTRATION

- Submitted daily **reports** to Systek, following inspection of work sites, reporting damage, equipment and materials needed, and tasks remaining to be done.
- **Interviewed** and **hired** gardeners for Systek.
- **Verified** and submitted weekly employee **time-sheets** for both CETA and Systek.
- **Coordinated** field trip arrangements for CETA workers: selected botanical sites to visit, and rearranged work schedules to accommodate special trips.
- Developed estimates for Systek landscape **contracts**.
- **Organized** retirement dinners for School District gardeners.
- Served on **negotiating** team for union contracts with Oakland School District.

LIAISON, COMMUNITY RELATIONS

- **Led tours** of Botanical gardens for student groups and garden clubs.
- Acted as **liaison** between gardeners and administrators, as union shop steward at Oakland Unified School District.
- Served as **liaison** between CETA gardeners, District teachers, and administrators.
- **Mediated** minor grievances and approved landscaping requests of Homeowners Association, as landscape maintenance supervisor for Systek contractors.

EMPLOYMENT HISTORY

1974-87	**Gardener/Assistant Foreman**	OAKLAND UNIFIED SCHOOL DIST., Oakland
	Gardener Caretaker, live-in	OAKLAND UNIFIED SCHOOL DISTRICT, Chabot Science Center
1972-74	**Landscape Maintenance Supv.**	SYSTEK, Landscaping Division, Concord (building contractors)
1971-72	**Head Gardener**	BROOKSIDE HOSPITAL, San Pablo
1960-71	**Nurseryman**	BOTANICAL GARDENS, U.C. Berkeley

EDUCATION & TRAINING

Horticulture course work, MERRITT COLLEGE
•Horticulture •Greenhouse Management •Plant Diseases •Herbicidious Plants

Horticulture Workshops, UCB BOTANICAL GARDENS:
•Plant Identification •Plant Maintenance •Propagating •Spraying

Supervisory Training, OAKLAND SCHOOL DISTRICT

Ed is exploring some new career directions that draw on his technical knowledge. Ed's Cover letter is on page 59.

EDMUND L. APITZ
2004 San Antonio Ave.
Alameda CA 94501
(415) 067-2441

Objective: Position as Buyer, with Northern California Mechanical Systems, Inc.

HIGHLIGHTS OF QUALIFICATIONS

★ Relate easily with all levels of personnel, from laborers to management.
★ Able to work under pressure and complete projects on time.
★ Experience specifying and recommending tools, equipment, materials.
★ Innovative in designing procedures relevant to materials.
★ Background and education in materials technology and machining.

RELEVANT EXPERIENCE

TECHNICAL EXPERTISE
- Specified and ordered materials and equipment used in machining, maintenance, and installations.
- Audited conditions of incoming finished and unfinished materials:
  - Set up a log of all incoming materials (tubings, fittings, machine parts, etc.)
  - Inspected contents; documented findings; reported to shipping authorities.
- Used schematics, blueprints, and manuals for machining of parts and maintenance of equipment.
- Performed welding, using gas and arc systems; supervised other welders.
- Operated engine lathes, milling machines, shapers, surface grinders, honing machines, cylinder grinders.

ADMINISTRATIVE
- Performed a cost evaluation, saving the company $15,000 by choosing local fabrication rather than overseas purchase.
- Set up an inventory system for $200,000 in spare parts.
- Researched potential markets for power generation maintenance services.
- Designed effective system to document maintenance history for Phillips Petroleum.
- Coordinated timely distribution of critical parts to repair sites for U.S. Navy and General Electric.

EMPLOYMENT HISTORY

1988-present	**Independent Contractor, Mechanical Equipment**	
1987-88	**Power Specialist**	POWER PLANT SERVICES, INC., Alameda CA
1976-86	**Field Service Rep**	GENERAL ELECTRIC CO., Schenectady NY and Evendale OH

EDUCATION

A.S., Materials Technology, LANEY JR. COLLEGE, Oakland CA
CONTINUING EDUCATION
Gas Turbine diploma, JETMA TECHNICAL INSTITUTE, San Francisco CA
Field Service Engineering diploma, GENERAL ELECTRIC, Schenectady NY
Maintenance Material Control diploma, U.S. NAVY

PROFESSIONAL AFFILIATIONS
- American Society for Metals
- American Welding Society

Action Verbs

The **underlined** words are especially good for pointing out **accomplishments**.

Management Skills
administered
analyzed
assigned
attained
chaired
consolidated
contracted
coordinated
delegated
developed
directed
evaluated
executed
improved
increased
organized
oversaw
planned
prioritized
produced
recommended
reviewed
scheduled
strengthened
supervised

Communication Skills
addressed
arbitrated
arranged
authored
collaborated
convinced
corresponded
developed
directed
drafted
edited
enlisted
formulated
influenced
interpreted
lectured
mediated
moderated

Communication (continued)
negotiated
persuaded
promoted
publicized
reconciled
recruited
spoke
translated
wrote

Research Skills
clarified
collected
critiqued
diagnosed
evaluated
examined
extracted
identified
inspected
interpreted
interviewed
investigated
organized
reviewed
summarized
surveyed
systematized

Technical Skills
assembled
built
calculated
computed
designed
devised
engineered
fabricated
maintained
operated
overhauled
programmed
remodeled
repaired

Technical (continued)
solved
upgraded

Teaching Skills
adapted
advised
clarified
coached
communicated
coordinated
demystified
developed
enabled
encouraged
evaluated
explained
facilitated
guided
informed
instructed
persuaded
set goals
stimulated
trained

Financial Skills
administered
allocated
analyzed
appraised
audited
balanced
budgeted
calculated
computed
developed
forecasted
managed
marketed
planned
projected
researched

Creative Skills
acted
conceptualized
created
customized
designed
developed
directed
established
fashioned
founded
illustrated
initiated
instituted
integrated
introduced
invented
originated
performed
planned
revitalized
shaped

Helping Skills
assessed
assisted
clarified
coached
counseled
demonstrated
diagnosed
educated
expedited
facilitated
familiarized
guided
motivated
referred
rehabilitated
represented

Clerical or Detail Skills
approved
arranged
catalogued
classified
collected
compiled
dispatched
executed
generated
implemented
inspected
monitored
operated
organized
prepared
processed
purchased
recorded
retrieved
screened
specified
systematized
tabulated
validated

More Verbs for Accomplishments
achieved
expanded
improved
pioneered
reduced (losses)
resolved (problems)
restored
spearheaded
transformed

Examples of some
Skill Areas

TRANSFERABLE SKILLS and SPECIAL KNOWLEDGE

The areas of Skill and Knowledge you choose to present on your resume are determined by what you think will be required of you in your new line of work. Here are some examples of Skill Areas presented by job hunters, along with the type of job they were looking for. (Remember, these are some POSSIBLE skill areas for those jobs — not necessarily the RIGHT ones for anybody else!)

The job: **School Counselor**
The skill areas presented:
—Individual counseling
—Testing and Evaluation
—Group Counseling
—Resource Development
—Career Development

The job: **Research Chemist**
The skill areas presented:
—Quality Control
—Project Management
—Analysis/R&D
—Instrument Knowledge

The job: **Substitute Teacher**
  (in an inner city school district)
The skill areas presented:
—Teaching
—Planning and Organizing
—Cultural/Racial Exposure
—Expertise in Math, Science, Health

The job: **Program Development**
  (with an elderly population)
The skill areas presented:
—Administration and Planning
—Elderly Services
—Community Services

The job: **Family Mediator**
The skill areas presented:
—Conflict Resolution
—Counseling and Interviewing
—Teaching and Educating

The job: **Fitness Consultant**
The skill areas presented:
—Athletic Training
—Individual Consultations
—Fitness Program Design and
  Implementation
—Personal Accomplishments
  (relevant awards he won)

The job: **Marketing and Public Relations**
The skill areas presented:
—Promotion
—Marketing
—Public Relations
—Customer Service/Needs Assessment

The job: **Sales Representative or
  Manufacturer's Rep**
The skill areas presented:
—Effective Sales Techniques
—Market Development
—Presentation/Communication

The job: **Commercial Leasing Agent**
The skill areas presented:
—Sales and Marketing
—Business Contacts
—Contract Negotiation
—Facilities Management

The job: **Receptionist**
The skill areas presented:
—Office Experience
—Telephone and Communication Skills
—Computer Knowledge

The job: **Private Investigator**
The skill areas presented:
—Investigation
—Case Management
—Security Consultation

The job: **Union Business Agent**
The skill areas presented:
—Contract Negotiations
—Grievance Handling and Contract
  Enforcement
—Organizing Workers
—Administration/Management

The job: **Information Specialist**
The skill areas presented:
—Information Needs Analysis
—Advising
—Research and Writing
—Data Management

The job: **Fire Fighter**
  (in a city fire department)
The skill areas presented:
—Crisis Evaluation and Response
—PR, Community Relations
—Medical Teamwork
—Training and Quality Assurance

The job: **Service Writer**
  (for an auto manufacturer)
The skill areas presented:
—Needs Assessment/Public Relations
—Technical Knowledge
—Business Management

The job: **Parish Minister**
The skill areas presented:
—Counseling and Pastoral Service
—Religious Education
—Worship
—Administration

The job: **Wardrobe Assistant**
  (with a movie company)
The skill areas presented:
—Managing Dressing Room
—Appointments/Logistics
—Costume Maintenance
—Bookkeeping, Shopping, Errands

The job: **Accountant**
  (with a computer firm)
The skill areas presented:
—Bookkeeping
—Computerized Accounting
—Computer Systems and Applications

The job: **Regional Planner**
The knowledge areas presented:
—Land Use
—Transportation
—Planning
—Economic Development

The job: **Massage Therapist**
  (free-lancing with a fitness center)
The skill areas presented:
—Non-Invasive Pain Control
—Sports Massage/Sports Therapy
—Assessment and Client Reeducation
—Professional Affiliations and Referrals

The job: **Program Administrator**
The skill areas presented:
—Administration/Management
—Program Development
—Special Projects
—Community Relations

The job: **Investigative Assistant**
The skill areas presented:
—Research
—Report Writing and Documentation
—Interviewing
—Data Entry

The job: **Staff Accountant**
The skill areas presented:
—Tax Planning
—Advising Management
—Trouble-Shooting
—Computer Conversion

The job: **Social Worker**
The skill areas presented:
—Clinical Counseling
—Assessment and Diagnosis
—Supervision/Administration
—Group Counseling
—Program Development

The job: **Doctor's Receptionist**
The skill areas presented:
—Office Skills
—Client Screening
—Client Relations

The job: **Assistant Manager Trainee**
  (in a restaurant)
The skill areas presented:
—Business Management
—Personnel, Supervision, Training
—Food Handling, Preparation, and
  Presentation

COVER LETTERS

Cover letters are EXTREMELY important. Whenever your resume is sent by mail, a cover letter should go along with it.

Here's what a Damn Good Cover Letter needs to accomplish:

1) **Address someone in authority** (by name and title) who could hire you. When it's IMPOSSIBLE to get that information, use a functional title ("Dear Manager") even if you have to guess ("Dear Selection Committee").

2) **Tell how you became attracted** to this particular company.

3) **Demonstrate that you've done some "homework"** on the company and can see THEIR point of view (their current problems, their interests, their priorities).

4) **Convey your enthusiasm and commitment** (even passion?) for this line of work.

5) **Balance professionalism with personal warmth and friendliness.** Avoid using generic, alienating phrases like "enclosed please find," or "Dear Sir." This is a PERSONAL letter.

6) **Identify at least one thing about you that's unique** — say, a special gift for getting along with all kinds of people — something that goes beyond the basic requirements of the position, that distinguishes you, AND is relevant to the position. (Then if several others are equally qualified there's a reason to pick YOU.)

7) **Be appropriate** to the field you're exploring — **stand out**, but in a non-gimmicky way.

8) **Outline specifically what you are asking** and offering.

9) **Point directly to the next step,** telling just what YOU will do to follow through.

10) **Remain as brief and focused as possible.**

This is NOT EASY to do! On the following pages are some examples of cover letters written by and with the author's clients. Nothing is "made up," but details may have been changed at the job hunter's request.

SAMPLE COVER LETTERS

NOTE: In all cases, the original cover letter included the DATE and the job hunter's RETURN ADDRESS AND PHONE NUMBER, which are removed here to save space.

Mr. Ralph Bunnell, Personnel
California Mechanical Systems
487 Industrial Park Drive
Richmond CA 94806

SEE RESUME ON PAGE 54

Dear Mr. Bunnell,

Through Experience Unlimited of Oakland, I learned of your opening for the position of Buyer, and spoke to you about it on October 20. As you requested, I am enclosing a resume outlining my experience as it relates to this position.

As you will note, I have 10 years of technical experience dealing with both customers and manufacturing management. I believe that my background combining very relevant technical and administrative skills would be of benefit in this position.

I would enjoy an in-person discussion of my qualifications and your needs, in more detail.

Sincerely,

Edmund L. Apitz

J.R. Baker, President
WASABE CYCLES
78 North Mountain Road
Schenectady NY 12305

SEE RESUME ON PAGE 45

Dear Mr. Baker,

I am enclosing a copy of my resume, which outlines my strengths in the areas of marketing support, field liaison, and research and development.

For the past 2-1/2 years I have worked for Point Reyes Bikes, which has earned a reputation for dealing with some of the finest domestic, hand-built bikes available. During that time, I have become familiar with all aspects of the retail bike business, in particular mountain bikes.

I am familiar with Wasabe's mountain bike components and use some of them on my own personal mountain and road bikes. In my opinion, your AB Gruppo was the most innovative mountain bike component package available at the time, clearly having a competitive edge. But for one reason or another, Wasabe seemed to take a back seat to the competition for awhile in the area of contemporary mountain bike components.

At this year's Reno trade show, however, I was pleased to notice that Wasabe seems to have gotten back in the running and I would like to be part of that comeback.

I feel I have much to offer due to my familiarity with top-of-the-line mountain bikes and components, and I would enjoy discussing these subjects with you, as well as my possible employment. I may be reached at home (415) 404-0900, or at work (415) 404-6776.

Sincerely,

William Majoué

Marjorie Lawrence, Director
Professional Training Institute
3056 Hildegard Ave.
Richmond CA 94806

SEE RESUME ON PAGE 50

Dear Ms. Lawrence,

The position of Marketing Trainer that you described in our meeting is an opportunity of great motivational and professional dimensions. I can envision a strong team atmosphere, working to achieve the Institute's goals, with an emphasis on commitment to the representatives' growth potential.

My attached resume will show that I have a strong training background. I believe I have a great deal to contribute to the department, given my experience and interest, as well as my sense of humor and creative energy.

I am very excited about the position. The people, functions, and environment all add up to a very appealing challenge. I look forward to talking with you in person.

Sincerely,

Maria Doshan

Coordinator of Certificated Personnel
1025 Second Avenue
Oakland CA 94606

SEE RESUME ON PAGE 46

Dear Coordinator,

I was very pleased to learn of the opening for the position of Principal at Oakland High School.

On my enclosed resume I have outlined my professional and educational background, and given special attention to those experiences and accomplishments that address Oakland High's stated needs and requirements.

I am a "take charge" type of administrator, and have demonstrated strong leadership and initiative in addressing the schools' most difficult problems. I have a particularly strong record of success in developing curriculum that meets the needs of all students.

It is my nature and philosophy to look for the best in students, and to do whatever is necessary to help them perform to their fullest potential. With this in mind, I recently attended a workshop at Harvard University (and plan to return this summer), where materials have been developed to effectively teach study skills to high school students. This workshop prepared me to introduce these critically important materials to teachers for use in their classrooms.

I would welcome the opportunity to share with you additional examples of contributions I might make to the program at Oakland High School.

Sincerely,

Ruben E. Lopez

STGC
Box 1282
41 Sutter St.
San Francisco CA 94104

SEE RESUME ON PAGE 28

Dear Selection Committee:

Because of my combined interest in accounting and computers, I am applying for the bookkeeper position which you recently advertised.

I am enclosing a copy of my resume for your consideration, and would like to call your attention to the areas of skill and achievement in my background that are most relevant.

—Over 12 years bookkeeping experience for a variety of businesses.

—Over 4 years full-charge bookkeeping experience with computerized accounting systems.

—Familiar with PC-DOS operating system.

—Exceptionally organized and resourceful, with a wide range of skills.

My current employer is gradually retiring from active law practice, and therefore I am looking for a new position. My current salary is $25,000 and I do not wish to earn less than that in my new job.

I would appreciate a personal interview with you to discuss my application further.

Sincerely,

Kate Dietrich

Customer Service Manager
FIRST UNITED BANK
28900 Foothill Blvd.
Oakland CA 94601

SEE RESUME ON PAGE 41

Dear Manager,

In response to your recent ad in the Oakland Tribune for a Customer Service Representative, I am enclosing my resume showing my past experience in customer service. As shown on my resume, I enjoy keeping busy and I am a dedicated hard worker.

Here are my business references and phone numbers as requested in your ad:

Mrs. Rebecca S. Kurle, 870-6160
Manager of Health Plans, Maplehurst Medical Group

Ms. Suzanne Amos, 870-6163
Assistant to Mrs. Kurle, Maplehurst Medical Group

Yana Parker, 540-5876
Owner, Damn Good Resume Service

You may call me at my home number, 614-2020, or leave a message at 907-3221. Thank you for your consideration, and I look forward to meeting you for an interview.

Sincerely,

Estelle Gade

TEN TOUGH QUESTIONS

About Resumes

1. "How do I account for that year when I wasn't employed?"

2. "What if I was 'just a housewife' for 20 years?"

3. "What do I do about dates on my job history . . . when I had two or three little jobs with a month or so in between?"

4. "What if I was called a 'secretary' and never got the pay or job title for all the things I really did?"

5. "Can't I just skip the Job Objective? I don't want to limit myself."

6. "What if I don't have any work experience in the exact job that I want now?"

7. "How long should a resume be? One page? Two?"

8. "What if my experience was from a long time ago?"

9. "What if they insist on a chronological resume and a lot of dates?"and finally . . .

10. "How should I use my resume?"

1. "HOW DO I ACCOUNT FOR THAT YEAR WHEN I WASN'T EMPLOYED?"

Tell the truth, creatively.

BE POSITIVE; refer to what you WERE doing rather than to what you WEREN'T doing. Don't say "unemployed" because it MIGHT convey an UN-truth about you, that you aren't interested in working, when in fact we both know you WANT to work. Instead, look at what you WERE doing, allow yourself a reasonable degree of "being human," and emphasize the positive aspects of what you did that year.

EXAMPLE: Candidly from my own experience . . . in 1974 I was traveling across the country "trying to figure out what to do with the rest of my life," coping with an unexpected traumatic illness, making some embarrassing and painful and wonderful experiments in "alternative lifestyles," and looking—sometimes desperately—for work that I could feel good about. I got by on unemployment for awhile, Medi-Cal for the illness, off-and-on Kelly Girl work, and loans from Mom. It was a very tough year.

What does it say on my resume?
"1974—Travel and independent study"
And that's true! I've just expressed it with more dignity than I was feeling at the time. I

don't need to tell anybody, on my resume, what a bummer that year was. And believe me, I learned enough to justify calling it "independent study"!

2. "WHAT IF I WAS 'JUST A HOUSEWIFE' FOR 20 YEARS?"

Change your attitude, for starters.

If you're a mother just entering or reentering the work force, don't discount your value with an apologetic approach. Replace the "housewife" image with "Family Management," or SOMETHING that expresses a woman's long-term commitment in this role with both honesty and dignity.

It's up to US to take the initiative here, to create a legitimate place in our "work history" for times when family responsibilities were top priority. (Besides childbirth and parenting, that may include periods needed to handle family illness, elderly parents, or death and settling an estate.) The response we get with this approach is greatly influenced by OUR OWN ATTITUDE, so keep it positive.

If you also did some substantial community work while your were "just a housewife," now is the time to discard the myth that only PAID work counts. Start listing everything of value that you accomplished, and an impressive body of skills, knowledge, and experience will emerge: fund-raising, program development, public relations, community organizing, counseling, teaching, writing, research.

The task then is to learn to express all this experience in world-of-work terms. Get help and support from places like "Displaced Homemaker" centers, Women's Centers, or community agencies, or college Career Centers, for the needed attitude change and help in analyzing your skills and writing about them.

3. "WHAT DO I DO ABOUT DATES ON MY JOB HISTORY? . . . WHEN I HAD TWO OR THREE LITTLE JOBS, WITH A MONTH OR SO IN BETWEEN?"

Omit very short-term jobs.

OR, combine several of them into one entry (for example if you did several similar jobs, briefly, for different employers, you could say "1981-82 Part-time Salesclerk. Macy's; Capwell's; Tradeway." It's still honest, yet it looks less fragmented.

Stick to YEARS rather than precise dates by-the-month. Rounding off to years keeps the reader from doing a lot of detailed arithmetic with your work record when you want them to focus on your SKILLS. Read the Employer Feedback section ('The Acid Test'); employers have differing opinions about this.

4. "WHAT IF I WAS CALLED A 'SECRETARY' AND NEVER GOT THE PAY OR THE JOB TITLE FOR ALL THE THINGS I REALLY DID?"

You don't HAVE to use THEIR job title! So MUCH fine and important work is done every day in millions of offices by intelligent women who aren't being adequately paid or acknowledged for the high levels of their skills and responsibilities.

"COME THE REVOLUTION . . ." Meanwhile, take the initiative to create a fairer job title that reflects the highest level of skills you used as a so-called "secretary."

EXAMPLE: One client's old resume listed "secretary" positions five times. Her new DAMN GOOD RESUME refers to those same jobs with the following reasonable, fair job titles:

> office supervisor
> director's assistant
> technical writer
> executive secretary
> administrative assistant

5. "CAN'T I JUST SKIP THE JOB OBJECTIVE? I DON'T WANT TO LIMIT MYSELF."

NO! Clearly stating your objective serves two vital purposes. The first is to FOCUS YOU (not to box you in); it's critically important to KNOW WHAT YOUR JOB OBJECTIVE IS, as explicitly as possible, and to have everything on your resume directly relate to it.

The second purpose is to inform the reader of your agenda—why this piece of paper is in her hand. That focus, clarity, and directness is what makes it a DAMN GOOD RESUME.

And remember, you could have TWO or more resumes, each with a different objective. The job search goes faster, however, when you focus hard on one objective at a time.

6. "WHAT IF I DON'T HAVE ANY WORK EXPERIENCE IN THE TYPE OF JOB I WANT TO DO NOW?"

The DAMN GOOD RESUME format is perfect for that situation. If you really want a particular kind of job and are sure you could do well at it if only you got the chance, it's just about certain that you have enough TRANSFERABLE skills to show that you're a good candidate for the job—at LEAST at the entry level.

Here's what your resume will need to show:

— Transferable skills from paid or unpaid experience.
— A credible progression from where you've been to where you want to go now. (If there's a leap the size of the Grand Canyon from where you are to the position you want, then be willing to state a current objective that bridges that gap.)
— Evidence of motivation and potential—experience that used the same kind of personality traits and strengths that your Ideal Job calls for.

TIP FOR STUDENTS WITH NO WORK EXPERIENCE

Students (both high school and college) sometimes think they have no work experience to put on their resume, until they look at the many informal ways they acquired skills that are actually marketable, for example:

- Working on a school paper or yearbook (researching, editing, writing, selling ads)
- Working as a student intern for a business
- Serving on student government committees
- Coaching sports or tutoring academic subjects
- Winning recognition for an exceptionally good essay, report, project
- Helping a professor research background information for a textbook
- Photography projects; science projects; marketing projects
- Helping to promote a concert
- Helping put a band together
- Helping with church activities
- Leadership in a club

Look at Stephen's resume on page 29 for more ideas.

7. "HOW LONG SHOULD A RESUME BE? ONE PAGE? TWO?"

One page is wonderful, one-and-a-half to two is also acceptable. Over two is NOT acceptable. Think of your resume as a marketing piece — it should be more like a billboard than like a phone book! Or think of it as a handful of aces . . . you DON'T deal out the whole deck! Prospective employers don't WANT your whole life history; they only need to see the essential points that make you qualified, plus the unique experience and attitudes that make you SPECIAL. So say the minimum, powerfully.

> The task is NOT to create a condensed version of your entire work life. Instead, it is to SELECT some of the MOST RELEVANT work experiences and accomplishments that support your current Job Objective.

8. "WHAT IF MY EXPERIENCE WAS FROM A LONG TIME AGO?"

With this format, the employer's attention is drawn toward your SKILLS (which appear first, and take up most of the space) rather than to the dates when you worked.

However, notice that we NEVER OMIT DATES (because that would undermine your credibility). You don't have to go ALL the way back, if the entire span of your work experience would indicate an age that's likely to result in discrimination. But once you start, leave no gaps from that point to the present.

9. "WHAT IF I'M TOLD I SHOULD USE A CHRONOLOGICAL RESUME?"

You could point out that your resume DOES include a chronological list of your work experience, even though you may not go into detail about the less relevant jobs.

OR, you may decide to go for the chronological format. Some knowledgeable folks say that a chronological resume is a good choice if you're staying in exactly the same field but moving up the ladder of responsibility.

In any case, your One-Liners should STILL focus on the activities, skills, and accomplishments most relevant to the FUTURE job. There are three chronological examples in this book: Ruben on page 46, Estelle on page 41, and Lorraine on page 40.

10. "HOW SHOULD I USE MY RESUME?"

a) **As a last-resort first contact**, when there's no way around it and you simply can't make the initial contact any other way. (A blind ad, for example.) But be creative . . . there often IS another way to reach the Hiring Person. Send an excellent cover letter along with the resume.

b) **Before your job interview**, to get you focused and clear. Tuck the resume in your pocket to look at just before you enter the new workplace; it will remind you of your skills and accomplishments, in case you tend to space out about them.

c) **To avoid filling out a job application** until after you've had a personal interview with the Hiring Person. Attach your resume to the application INSTEAD of filling out the Employment History section, which is invariably designed to your disadvantage. You DO NOT have to give all that information before being interviewed. (EXCEPTION: for civil service jobs, your application won't even get processed unless you fill out the application fully. In THAT case, don't fight it . . . do it THEIR way!)

d) **After your interview**, you can leave it with the employer as a concrete reminder and documentation of the information you provided during the interview. DO NOT hand it to the employer at the beginning of your meeting; she'll be looking at the resume instead of at YOU!

e) **On an "Informational Interview"** (see p. 23) when you're researching a new career direction, show your draft resume and ask for advice on how to improve it, and whether all the important issues are covered.

f) **Among your friends and family**, so they know what you're looking for and what your skills are; they can keep an eye out for job leads.

"UPGRADE RESUME" IDEA:
MOVE UP/MOVE ON, WITHOUT MOVING OUT!

Do you feel stuck or dissatisfied with your job? It's worth a try to bid for an upgrade with your current employer, even if there's no apparent place to go. Create a Damn Good Resume showing your value to the company, and propose an upgrade in responsibility and salary. Brook's "upgrade resume" on page 37 outlined some problem-solving ideas he was willing to implement, and was well received by his managers.

THE ACID TEST

What Do Employers Think About Resumes?

In this edition, we UPDATE our chapter on employer feedback about resumes. Here's advice and comments from a NEW panel of nine Bay Area employers.

First, an introduction to the nine employers:

"DC" is an employment recruiter for a bank with thousands of employees.

"JD" is director of training programs at a community career center employing five people.

"KJ" is a recruiter for county civil service jobs in hospitals, clinics, health agencies.

"MM" recruits professionals for an engineering-related company with 11,000 employees.

"RS" is a personnel and training director for a software company with 200 employees.

"RV" is executive director of a small nonprofit agency.

"SP" recruits for a construction company with 50,000 employees worldwide.

"AA" hires local staff for a large toy manufacturer and distributor.

"SB" hires secretaries, janitors, and maintenance staff for a large pharmaceutical firm with 10,000 employees.

As you read their comments, you may want to refer back to the outline above for perspective on their views.

We showed the employers seven resumes that appear in this book (all seven job-hunters, by the way, did succeed in getting interviews using these resumes):

Notice how differently employers approach resumes! Some look at them conservatively, others with a "guerrilla tactics" approach. Some like specific objectives, others prefer general. Perhaps the most controversial are the subjective, self-marketing statements — they either love 'em or they hate 'em.

And notice that EMPLOYERS DON'T ALWAYS AGREE. So you obviously can't please everybody all the time! On the other hand, THIS panel is virtually unanimous on some points — for example, they're all turned off by pretentious, commercially prepared resumes.

Notice, too, that although each of these seven sample resumes WORKED to get an interview for the job hunter, employers still found some areas that could be improved, in addition to the things they liked. Ruben's resume in particular generated some controversy and diverse opinions. We chose to LEAVE the resumes "as is" (with one exception as noted) so you readers could see just what the employers were criticizing or praising.

1. HOW DO YOU DECIDE
WHETHER IT'S A GOOD RESUME?

DC: The objective is the key; that gets it to the right person, the appropriate hiring manager. It also needs to look nice, as though you've taken some time with it. And keep it to one or two pages.

JD: The most important thing is to focus on what you're seeking. And show that you understand the main qualifications of the job, rather than just showing your past job experience. Make it easy for the recruiter — don't use jargon that the average lay person can't understand.

KJ: The format and presentation are important; and show what functions you have performed, along with your job history.

MM: Conciseness — a resume that makes for quick reading and that supports your interest areas; also that shows you take pride in your work.

RS: I look for how easy it is to read, how apparent the qualifications are in a quick scan. The objective needs to stand out.

RV: Is it targeted to the job and to the most critical skill area of the job? It should take the reader by the hand: "This is what I've done and where I've done it, and these are the achievements to back up what I'm applying for."

SB: It needs to look good on the page, and have a pretty specific objective, otherwise I won't read it. I also don't read it if it says "Looking for a position with a company that will allow me to use wonderful, fabulous skills." Instead I want to see "Looking for a middle management position in finance," etc.

SP: I look for experience (particularly experience with the competition) and a good education.

AA: I go by its general appearance — also the specific qualifications for the position being recruited.

2. WHAT MAKES YOU DECIDE THAT THIS LOOKS LIKE SOMEBODY YOU WOULD LIKE TO INTERVIEW?

DC: If I see action words and accomplishments rather than just job descriptions, that's when I get excited about interviewing. Also if there's something in the cover letter that attracts my attention, that shows time and thought and effort, and some real interest in our organization.

JD: If the person is very sure of what they want to do and what contribution they can make. Our bank needs self-starters so we're looking for demonstrated initiative.

KJ: If the skills and functions on the resume are appropriate and well presented.

MM: If the education and experience are a good match for the position we have open. [AA agrees.]

RS: The person's background looks good and there's no big gaps in their history. I like to see clear objectives, qualifications, and continuity in the job history. (If you took time off, then clearly state the reason.)

RV: Show that you know the lingo of the environment; for example in sales, your resume should reflect that you know how to close.

SB: The resume writer has no control over this because our candidates have to meet a manager's particular requirements — for example, having worked with the "Big Eight" or having an MBA.

   With secretaries it's not so cut-and-dried; then I'll look for skills listed at the top of the resume: typing, shorthand, software packages, etc., and then look at the job history to see if she's a job hopper. (Of course things are changing — because people get laid off.)

SP: I pay the most attention when the objective is for a specific position that relates to the job hunter's skills.

3. WHAT DO YOU CONSIDER MOST IMPORTANT ON A RESUME?

DC: The objective. Plus dates when things happened, and accomplishments.

JD: Knowing what you want to do and what contribution you could make.

KJ: Valid information in an easy-to-read, attractive style.

RS: A clear objective, backed up with qualifying experience and continuity in the work history.

RV: Realizing that the employer is looking for "red flags" and making sure there aren't any; cover gaps in dates, cover duties, eliminate suspicions and questions.

SB: The presentation and the objective.

SP: The address and phone number! Lots of people only put them in the cover letter!

AA: Meeting the qualifications for the job.

4. WHAT TURNS YOU OFF ON A RESUME?

DC: Personal data — that's a major "red flag." Typos, inconsistent punctuation, lack of address and phone number. And huge paragraphs that look like job descriptions, without any skills and accomplishments pulled out.

JD: Those odd-size resumes from resume services, saying "Presenting the candidacy of . . ." Also personal information, and resumes that sound like job descriptions. Also, not looking at the employer's needs, not doing any research.

KJ: Those portfolio things on parchment paper, from a resume service. They look so fake and phony, an instant turnoff.

MM: Omissions in terms of dates, and misspellings.

RS: Long cover letters and resumes more than two pages long.

RV: Excess cosmetics, substituting form for content. It should look nice, but don't go overboard; it's a traditional tool and it should look traditional.

SB: Resumes that open like a book, saying "Presenting so-and-so," done by a commercial resume service. They're just a rip-off and I don't even read them anymore.

SP: A photo; I have to remove them because a manager should be color blind and gender blind. Also not sending the resume to the right place.

AA: Misspelled words, poor grammar, a messy look.

5. WHAT WOULD YOU LIKE TO SEE DIFFERENT ON RESUMES THAT WOULD HELP EMPLOYERS IDENTIFY A GOOD CANDIDATE?

DC: I want to see people doing a good selling job talking about what they've done and accomplished. And I want to get the essence of the person, a feeling for their personality. (Sometimes people are too regimented as to what they think they "should" be saying about themselves.)

JD: Fewer chronological resumes. Less about job history and more about skills that apply to the job.

KJ: Resumes that are easy to read and understand, and that validate your background.

MM: Being real candid about what responsibility you've held, and what you're proud of accomplishing in that position. That lets me see where your values are. Also conciseness. (People have a misconception about resumes; they're really just a tickler, not the place to give the whole story away.)

RS: Resumes on one page, or 1-1/2 at most — brief and concise.

RV: I'd like to see job hunters incorporate their problem-solving skills right into the resume. For example "We had a problem with attendance and this is what we did to resolve it." That's probably a little visionary, but it would give me an idea of how they think and what their management style is.

SB: Don't be too splashy. There's nothing wrong with good white paper; in fact it's better because it makes better copies. Be honest and clear, and be grammatically correct and consistent.

AA: In the employment history I'd like to see the months included along with the years. And no highlights section — just the objective, education, and experience.

SP: Be honest and give some objective information rather than subjective self-evaluation.

6. HOW WOULD YOU REACT TO ANY OF THESE SEVEN JOB HUNTERS' RESUMES IF YOU WERE HIRING FOR THAT KIND OF WORK? DO YOU HAVE ANY COMMENTS, PRO OR CON?

JOHN REED's resume, *page 44*

DC: I like the highlights; they mention his professional manner with customers and then the skill section goes on to show how he has done this. This approach highlights a person's strengths and style and can work for almost everybody.

JD: It's easy to read and very clear.

KJ: I'd rather see his highlights in a cover letter when they include subjective things such as interpersonal skills, because the cover letter is the appropriate place for a sales pitch. I like that it's one page and gives me functions and skills.

MM: I like the objective. I'd suggest pushing the education up to the top. (I'd probably call him first to see why, all of a sudden, he wants to make this move; then if that made sense, I'd schedule him for a test.)

RS: I like it on one page. He should move the education and training to the top because most of his work was in restaurant management. In the job history, I'd change it to "1968-present: Consultant" or "1968-83: Waiter, and 1983-87: Consultant to Restaurant Management." These are guerrilla or street-fight tactics.

SB: I'd recommend putting the education up nearer to the objective, and of course including a good cover letter.

JOSEPHINE TRICKLER's resume, *page 49*

JD: This resume is right on target because it answers my questions with relevant skill areas presented in a hierarchy — customer service, supervision, and then administration. The objective is short, concise, and specific. And the summary tells me the qualities that relate to the three areas listed below: it shows that she's honest and reliable and productive, and consistently pleasant to customers.

KJ: I like it. Very tight, attractive format, and the skills are clearly pulled out. I like the "summary of qualifications" better than "highlights of qualifications" elsewhere.

MM: If everybody could do a resume on one page it would be perfect.

RS: I don't think she needs a functional resume.

RV: I appreciate the amount of white space.

AA: Good appearance. But again, what did she do as a retail clerk?

SP: Very good layout.

KATE DIETRICH's resume, *page 28*

DC: It's important to back up the objective, and Kate does that when she talks about her computer expertise. I also like to see it all on one page like that.

JD: I like this resume a lot. I especially like the reduced type here because you can see all the information without turning the page.

KJ: I like seeing the skills pulled out like this, rather than having to go through a work chronology and have to figure out what her skills are.

MM: It helps a lot, from the interviewer's perspective, that she goes into detail about what she knows and doesn't know. I like the layout and also the more specific objective. I'd have trouble with the number of positions she's listed and I'd want to cover that question with her right away.

SP: The overall layout leads you through it. I like seeing the computer experience that's appropriate to the job. And it's good to see the continuing education under her college degree.

   The work history is clear, though it's a bit scattered and I'd probably call her up to see if she's been laid off or was moving to improve her salary.

MARIA DOSHAN's resume, *page 50*

JD: It's easy to read and very clear; she has kept her extensive background concise by using a functional resume.

KJ: She could use smaller type and get it all on one page so I could see everything at one time. The objective is too limited, and I'd rather see that in a cover letter.

MM: I like it, even though it's different from my style in that it's so specific to one company. I like the highlights and the one-liners — really concise. What she brings out on the first page is nailed down on the second page.

SB: I don't like the comment "Keen intuition; warm, sincere, down-to-earth teaching style." But I do like "Designed and presented seminars for hospital middle-managers;" it's honest, it's something she actually DID, and it's objective information rather than subjective self-evaluation. I've never liked highlights. I like the old fashioned kind of resume. I want to know where and when you did something.

   Don't put in irrelevant information — for example, Maria's dramatics teaching. In the corporate world I've learned there's no connection between training and teaching.

ROBERT VENTURI's resume, *page 52*

RS: I think this resume has too much information — it should be readable in 30 seconds.

MM: The directed objective looks solid. I would switch the "park technical experience" to the front, but find this resume very interesting. [Editor's note: We took MM's advice and moved "park technical experience" from page two to page one.]

RUBEN LOPEZ's resume, *page 46*

RS: This is a good example in terms of quick readability. Ruben is using what I call "guerrilla tactics" in not emphasizing his latest jobs, but focusing on the three years at Union High School. (You can also emphasize one part of your experience if you're going for a job change that requires that experience.) Ruben could make a brief comment to explain why he went into corporate management.

DC: It's good that he has stressed what's important to him. I'm not sure it makes sense for him to do his resume in a chronological style — it's not as smooth as the others. On the other hand it looks good and says what he wants to get across. It's maybe too slanted toward his assistant principal job. My gut level question is, what did he do from 1983-85?

MM: I like it a lot — this is more my style. I like the combination format; it's a nice way to present himself, with the positions highlighted and also the action words in terms of what he's done.

KJ: The one-liners seem to take up too much space. I don't want to go through a chronology and have to figure out what the skills are; I'd rather see the skills pulled out like they are on Kate's or Josephine's resumes.

RV: I think the boxes detract from the highlights and make the dates stand out too much. [KJ, DC, AA, SB, and JD all disliked the boxes too.]

SB: Putting the education first is a good idea.

AA: Looks good; the combination format answers questions.

LORRAINE CHAPMAN's resume, *page 40*

AA: I like this because it is a combination of both chronological and functional, with the skills for the position described. And it looks good. I'd like to see the skills for her last position also, and know whether she's still there. [Editor's note: Lorraine was still employed there at the time this resume was written in 1987.]

DC: The boxes I think are nice but some people might think it's too much. On the other hand, since she works for media it could make sense to look flashy.

RS: Ideal — you can go right to the job history.

MM: Nice layout. I like the education at the end and "graduate cum laude." It's good to show things you're proud of; it shows you like yourself.

MORE EMPLOYER COMMENTS AND ADVICE FOR JOB HUNTERS

FORMATS: FUNCTIONAL vs. CHRONOLOGICAL

RS: I don't like functional resumes because I want to know where a person did what. But a functional format is good if you've had lots of jobs. In that case, my idea would be to use a "guerrilla approach," i.e., drop jobs and extend others "as long as your rear is covered." The most important thing is "getting on the beach," getting an interview. It's important to present a good image, but don't lie about your skills — don't say you can do something you can't do.

SB: An organization of recruiters I belong to, PYRA, believes that you do a functional resume when you have something to hide. However, sometimes a functional resume is good when you're doing a career change — or when you need to emphasize a part of your experience where you indeed don't HAVE that much experience but you still want to move into that area. (I did that kind of resume myself. But still, I like the old fashioned kind of resume.)

JOB OBJECTIVES

RS: I like more general objectives ("using my skills in finance . . . ") just in case there's both an accountant opening and another financial position.

SP: Don't make a generalized comment such as "desire challenging position." I will skip right over it. I pay the most attention when the objective is for a specific position based on the job hunter's skills.

MM: The more specific you are, the more likely you are to get what you want. The recruiter can then head you in the right direction.

COVER LETTERS

MM: I have a tendency to take a quick look at a resume and then go to the cover letter to see why they came to us, what they're interested in, what they're doing, so I can look at the resume in a more focused way. I use the cover letter to start seeing what kind of attitude a person has toward work.

SB: If there's anything unusual about your resume, you need a cover letter. (I always read the ones with cover letters first.) A good cover letter could say, for example, "I've been an office manager for several years at one company but I don't want to put in so much overtime and I'm looking for a stable job in a stable company where I can work 8 to 5." Ordinarily I wouldn't interview someone for a secretarial job after they've been an office manager, but now she's telling me WHY, so I'll bring her in.

DC: A cover letter should highlight something about you or do something else to attract my attention. It should show time and thought and effort — like you're really interested in our organization.

OVERALL IMPRESSION

DC: A resume is a marketing tool, like a beautiful brochure, creating an image of professionalism. Real gut level, these resumes look nice, like someone has taken some time. They use a lot of action words with short sentences that say something — the ideal type of resume, all in two pages.

MM: These resumes flow and move smoothly, so it's easy to jump around and not lose sight of what you're reading.

CHECK ✓ LIST
FOR BUILDING OR EVALUATING
A DAMN GOOD RESUME

A. FOCUS: Job Objective

☐ 1. Is the Job Objective included?

☐ 2. Is the Objective brief, clear, unambiguous?

☐ 3. Is it phrased in the appropriate language of that industry?

☐ 4. Does the Objective focus on the end-goal, rather than on the process of getting there? ("A position as _____," not "To seek a position as _____.")

☐ 5. Is the Objective presented from the employer's perspective? (not " . . . where I can use my/get my/have my . . . "

☐ 6. Is the Objective a realistic next step? (If not, is there another Objective that could form a "bridge" to it?)

B. ORGANIZATION, Coherence, Consistency

☐ 7. Does each part support and agree with the other parts? (for example, do the One-Liners effectively document the Highlights?)

☐ 8. Can you find all the DATES immediately?. . . and the JOB TITLES? . . . and the WORK PLACES?

☐ 9. Can you scan and find key words and action verbs near the start of each line?

C. RELEVANCE to the stated objective

☐ 10. Does the choice of skills presented reflect an understanding of the desired job?

☐ 11. Is the content limited to information that is clearly relevant? (documenting either job-content skills or special knowledge)

D. APPEAL . . . to the employer

Graphic appeal
☐ 12. Is there enough white space? (or does the text feel too dense?)

☐ 13. Is the content clustered into paragraphs? (not just run on and on)

☐ 14. Is the type style super easy to read and attractive?

Personal appeal
☐ 15. Does the job hunter sound real, warm, personable, unique?

☐ 16. Are there clues about her work values and professional motivation?

☐ 17. Does the work-related content sound interesting? Is it "alive"?

☐ 18. DOES IT WORK?!! Overall, could it make you want to meet this person?

E. APPEAL . . . to the job hunter

☐ 19. Does the resume REFRAIN from presenting skills the job hunter disliked using and doesn't want to use in the future? (that is, does it support her search for appropriate, satisfying work?)

☐ 20. **Does the job hunter feel proud, pleased, appreciated, and well represented, looking at her resume?**

©1989 Yana Parker, Damn Good Resume Service, Berkeley CA

INDEX

ANSWERING AN AD IN THE NEWSPAPER

When you apply for an advertised job, your Job Objective at the top of your resume should read word-for-word the same as the employer's job title. (I would even include the name of the company if I knew it.)

For the body of your resume (Highlights, Skills, One-Liners) the job announcement itself is an excellent guide. It usually outlines the basic abilities, special knowledge, and experience you need to talk about.

Be sure to respond to everything mentioned in the announcement. If you volunteer any more information, be sure it's actually relevant and is based on an accurate understanding of the nature of the job.

If at all possible, take time to do a little research on both the company and the position before you finalize the resume and cover letter.

About the Author

DAMN GOOD RESUME SERVICE
● (510) 540-5876

The author works in Berkeley, doing one-to-one resume counseling and writing, on a Macintosh computer. She also teaches and supervises a team of Damn Good Resume Writers-in-Training. Job hunters living in the San Francisco Bay Area can call the number above for information or an appointment.

HELP FOR NEW RESUME WRITERS

Yana provides support and training in the *business* of writing resumes, helping career counselors, entrepreneurs, retirees, and others to explore the career potential of full-time or part-time resume writing.

● Saturday or weekend workshops in the Bay Area.
● Newsletter, "Resume Pro Newsletter" issued two to four times a year.
● Phone consultation.

Call (510) 540-5876 or write to the address above.

IN-HOUSE TRAINING FOR PROFESSIONALS

Yana also presents in-house staff training workshops on resume writing for professionals in San Francisco Bay Area agencies, both corporate and nonprofit. If you would like her to work with your staff, please call. Or write **P.O. Box 3289, Berkeley, CA 94703.**

The disk contains:

- Templates in a variety of sharp looking design layouts for each of the four most useful resume configurations:
  - Chronological   - Functional   - Combined Chronological/Functional   - Accomplishment

  Each template has built-in step-by-step directions for what to say in every section of the resume, and the formatting and placement are already done for you. (Just type over the existing text with your own words.)

- Templates and models for special purpose resumes and letters, including:
  - Information Interviews
  - Job Promotions and Change of Status
  - Recommendation Letters
  - Cover Letters
  - Thank You Letters

- All of the above provided in one or more of the most popular word processing programs.

The 48-page manual provides:

- "Hard-copy" illustrations of all the resume templates.

- Very simple and complete instructions **for job hunters** on using ReadyToGo Resumes templates — including the features and advantages of each format, and how to choose the best layout for your situation.

- Guidelines **for professional resume writers, career counselors, educators, word processors**, and other professionals on how to use the Templates with your customers or clients.

- "Problem Patches" to handle problems such as:
  - Complex work history
  - No experience
  - Major career change
  - Erratic work experience
  - Time out for parenthood and family issues
  - Period of unemployment

- Eight sample resumes designed in the ReadyToGo Resumes formats.

NOTE: WordPerfect and Microsoft Word are registered trademarks of (respectively) WordPerfect Corp. and Microsoft Corp.)

Order Form

Please send "ReadyToGo Resumes" @ $39.95

Quantity		Cost
☐	IBM PC Compatible 3.5" disk (in WordPerfect <u>and</u> Microsoft Word) *Yes, it works with "Windows"*	_____
☐	IBM PC Compatible 5.25" disk (in WordPerfect <u>and</u> Microsoft Word)	_____
☐	Macintosh 3.5" disk (Microsoft Word) (write for availability of other formats)	_____
	Add **$3.50* per item for shipping** (* $4.00 to Canada)	_____

☐ Check here if you want info about a Newsletter for Resume Writers

Total: $ _____

Mail your order and payment to:
Yana Parker
(software department #10)
P.O. Box 3289
Berkeley CA 94703

Ship to:

Name _____

Title/Company _____

_____

Street _____

City _____

State _____ Zip _____

Phone (_____) _____

Method of Payment (US currency only):
☐ Corporate Purchase Order. PO# _____
☐ Check or Money Order **payable to Yana Parker**

P.S. At your local bookstore there's more help from Yana:
- *Damn Good Resume Guide*
- *The Resume Catalog: 200 Damn Good Examples*
- *Resume Pro: The Professional's Guide*